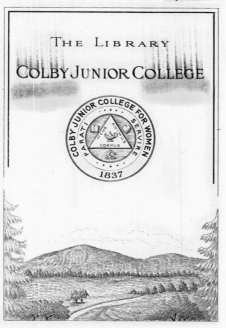

English Institute

Essays ⚘ 1946

English Institute Essays · 1946

The
Critical Significance of
Biographical Evidence;
The Methods of
Literary Studies

❧

NEW YORK · COLUMBIA UNIVERSITY PRESS · 1947

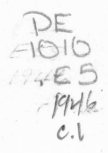

In Memoriam

C. F. TUCKER BROOKE

Editorial Committee

Preface

PERHAPS no explanation is necessary for the long interval between volumes four and five of the *English Institute Annual;* but for the record a simple statement of the facts may be worth while. Because of wartime conditions no meeting could be held after the short week-end of September 5 to 7, 1942, until September, 1946. With the ending of hostilities, the Institute met again—this time from the ninth through the 13th of September with an attendance of 169.

In the earlier *English Institute Annuals* selected papers from all conferences were included, no attempt being made to present a volume with a unified theme. This year, in contrast, only papers from two closely connected groups are printed—discussions of the various methods of literary scholarship and of the critical significance of biographical evidence. With interrelated themes, these essays should prove valuable to all who are interested in modern literary criticism.

As in the past, we wish to express appreciation to Columbia University, especially to Professor Ernest Hunter Wright and Mr. Philip Hayden, for continued hospitality and help.

Thanks are due also to the Columbia University Press for friendly cooperation in continuing the *English Institute Annual* series.

New York   *The Editorial Committee*
June, 1947

Contents

x   Contents

PART I

The Critical Significance of Biographical Evidence

Introduction

By G. E. BENTLEY

THE FAMILIAR ASSERTION in recent years that the study of English literature has been mostly a study of the lives of writers with little attention to their writings, that biographical studies have little relevance for the understanding of literature, that critical principles and their application should be the prime concern of students of literature, prompted the selection of the general subject for this series of papers. We hoped that if four scholars each examined the relevance of biographical facts in the understanding of the literary work of one particular writer of stature, we might, through their papers and the succeeding discussions, clarify somewhat our ideas of the use and abuse of biographical evidence. The papers here published on Milton, Swift, Shelley, and Yeats constituted the formal part of our program.

The scholars who have here examined the critical significance of biographical evidence have not, of course, produced a formula. They have neither espoused the extreme of the critical school which contends that nothing outside the text itself has any relevance for the student, nor proclaimed fuller biographical knowledge as the greatest need of literary studies. Their principal point of agreement seems to be that critics of Milton, Swift, Shelley, and Yeats have misused biographical evidence; that writers have turned "biographical conjecture into biographical fact"; that relevant biographical evidence has been ignored; that autobiographical interpretations have been overdone.

The principal significance of these papers is not to be sought, however, in their general agreement or disagreement on problems of the use of evidence. Each makes a contribution to the literature of its field. The reader, like the members of the English Institute, is offered an aid in his understanding of Milton, of Swift, of Shelley, and of Yeats.

John Milton

ༀ

By DOUGLAS BUSH

IN TRYING to assess the value of biographical evidence
for the understanding of Milton's poetry, we may
start with two or three obvious general facts.[1] Thanks
to Milton's own writings, the early biographers, and
the labors of Masson and modern scholars, we know
more about him than we know about any other Englishman of his century, or indeed about any Englishman before him. Moreover, to put much the same fact
in a different way, Milton was not an innocent by-
stander but an active revolutionary, and his poetry is
far outweighed in bulk by his prose writings. The
most direct and valuable insights into his life, character, and work are, of course, given by the autobiographical material in both prose and verse; and the
whole body of his prose, as the fullest record of his intellectual and spiritual development, is very important in itself and forms the best introduction to
and commentary upon his major poems. But I am as-

[1] This paper was originally written for delivery only and has been
abridged and somewhat revised for publication.

suming that the framers of this program were concerned with Milton's poetry and took his prose writings for granted.

Milton's public career and prose works have contributed a good deal to prejudice against the man and
the thinker and, consequently, against the poet. He
has in fact been a signal, perhaps a unique, victim of
the physical law enunciated by his great contemporary
—that pressure exerted anywhere upon a mass of fluid
is transmitted undiminished in all directions, and so
forth. For instance, the author of "Methought I saw
my late espoused Saint" has been charged with "a
Turkish contempt of females," although he only
shared the general and traditional view of woman's
inferiority to man in the chain of being, and although
he held an uncommonly high view of man, woman,
and marriage. He has suffered from the traditional
belief that he wrote his first tract on divorce during his
honeymoon; but modern investigation, especially by
Mr. B. A. Wright, of the merely circumstantial accounts of his marriage, has yielded virtual proof that it
occurred in 1642 and not a year later, so that one un-
lovely blot has been wiped out. Then, Milton being
by definition a great egoist and rebel, it has been said
again and again that his pamphlets were not disinterested but were the products of personal grievances.
Obviously Milton's personal feelings were involved, as
personal feelings are involved in any earnest attempt
to sway the public mind; but modern scholarship has
considerably modified this evidence of "egoism" by

showing that Milton was dealing with subjects to which he had earlier given disinterested thought.

These are only a few random—and mild—examples of the bits of mud which have been thrown so freely at Milton and which, coalescing, have provided the common and forbidding image of a great man with feet of clay. Whatever Milton's actual faults of character, it is a curious thing that his high and rare measure of virtue and righteousness causes much more offense than the scarlet sins of other writers. Literary critics can condemn the man without any evidence at all, and some scholars have been moved to magnify or manufacture evidence. Since the worst charges have been amply refuted, and indeed refute themselves, we need not go into them. I bring up the matter partly because, as I said, prejudice against Milton's personal character has colored so much criticism, and partly because it raises the large general question of how far the integrity of the man is bound up with the integrity of the artist. There are many critics and scholars who would apparently deny any relation between the two (except of course in regard to Milton). I myself hold the perhaps naïve belief that the integrity of the artist is not independent of the integrity of the man, though in saying that I do not mean to say what would be still more naïve, that integrity means moral blamelessness. But it seems to me no less naïve to assume, as a good many critics seem to do, that a shabby or dissolute life and character are a kind of guarantee of artistic integrity and that virtue is a fatal impediment. In the present instance, if we were forced to believe that Milton was a knave, or even a self-righteous hypocrite, I do not see how the religious and moral edifice of his poetry could stand unshaken. There are no doubt many poets, from Villon to Baudelaire and Hart Crane, who may in hell conceive a heavenly vision, but Milton is not of that kind; he is all of a piece.

To turn to the poetry, we may observe how biographical evidence has been used by a few critics and scholars. The first name that comes to mind is Dr. Johnson. Everyone knows both how greatly, at times, Johnson could write of Milton, and also how far his view of the man and the pamphleteer was colored by Anglican and Tory prejudice. He saw Milton as a proud egoist, a misguided and violent rebel against the church, a surly and acrimonious republican. But Johnson, whether right or wrong, was always an honest critic as well as an honest man. The notorious errors and defects in his account of Milton's poetry are not caused by the carrying over of personal, religious, and political prejudice into criticism; they come rather from want of sensibility and perception, a want aggravated by some articles of his literary creed.

If we jump down to the nineteen twenties and nineteen thirties, we find a hue and cry against Milton, led by such poets as Mr. Pound and Mr. Eliot and supported by their critical followers and a few others.[2] I recently gave some discussion to this subject in a small

[2] In incidental comments Mr. Eliot has been moving away from his earlier position and in his recent lecture on Milton he makes a considerable retraction.

book on *Paradise Lost* and cannot repeat it here. But we may remind ourselves briefly that this criticism was not at all disinterested; it started with the object of dethroning Milton in favor of "metaphysical" poets, from Dante and Donne to Pound and Eliot. Although modern criticism professes a lofty concern with an author's works and not his personal character, in the criticism of Milton no holds were barred. A prejudice against the man was used as a ready and easy way to establish a prejudice against his poetry. Milton was presented as a powerful but repellent personality who expounded repellent beliefs and ideas in verse of repellent organization and texture. Most of the dicta—one cannot call them arguments—directed against the man and the thinker were taken over uncritically from the nineteenth century; the only novelty was a dislike of the Miltonic style which the nineteenth century had glorified as sublime. Outside of this small but very assertive movement there were, of course, disinterested critics concerned only with understanding Milton's art, but it was the critics in the movement who had the ear of the highbrow reader.

If literary scholars have not approached such extremes of hostile prejudice, they have not always been proof against their own idols of the cave. For instance, M. Saurat's Milton, as I think Mr. Tillyard has remarked somewhere, comes to seem very much like a nineteenth-century French anticlerical. We may look somewhat closely at Saurat's work because he was a conspicuous exemplar of the use of biographical evidence and because he took a provocative and im-

portant part in the revaluation of Milton. The early
twentieth century inherited the romantic and nineteenth-century habit of ignoring or disparaging Milton's beliefs and ideas in order to "save" the poetry.
When the anti-Miltonist critics were summarily de-
nouncing Milton's beliefs and ideas in good set nineteenth-century terms, they were, as I said, rather out of
date. Such scholars as Greenlaw and Mr. Hanford had
been expounding the rich significance of Milton's
thought, and Saurat's book of 1925 gave wider currency to the new conception of Milton as a bold son
of the Renaissance rather than a rigid son of the Ref-
ormation, a humanist rather than a grim Puritan. It
was desirable that the pendulum should swing in that
direction, even if it went too far. But we are concerned
only with Saurat's use of biographical evidence, and
may take account of what appear to be some fundamental aberrations.

In the first place Saurat sees Milton as above all a
great heretic and proud independent rebel. Hence the
poet of *Paradise Lost,* even though he condemns Satan,
"pours out his own feelings" into the rebellious arch-
angel, who is part not only of his own character but of
his own mind. To take that view—which has, of course,
in some form or other been the common post-Roman-
tic view—is to make nonsense of the poem. One might
as well say that Shakespeare poured his own feelings
into Iago and Edmund and Macbeth.

Secondly, Saurat made Milton's first marriage the
focal point of his whole life and work—as, about the
same time, critics were making Wordsworth's French

affair the focal center of his life and work. In his marriage, according to Saurat, the chaste and prayerful Milton was carried away by his senses and soon recognized with pain and sorrow that he, the dedicated servant of God, had betrayed his spiritual self. And he never got over the shock of his experience, with the knowledge that it brought of the strength of masculine passion and of feminine allurements. Even Milton's monistic metaphysical ideas are said to start from this conflict.

Now we can justly infer that Milton found he had made a grievous mistake, and we may assume that in his as in any other marriage the senses had a natural share. It is possible that Saurat's account of the marriage and its consequences is an account of what happened. But the fact is that we do not have the evidence. And the chief trouble is not so much that Saurat turns biographical conjecture into biographical fact, but that he makes this conjecture the basis of much of his analysis of the later poems, *Paradise Lost* in particular. Mary Powell is the weak, frivolous, and seductive Eve, and Adam is the rational and religious Milton led astray by passion; and when Adam and Eve are reconciled, we witness the reunion of Milton and his wife. Again it is logically possible that Milton's early experience entered into the poem; but, in view of the traditional and universal interpretation of the fall, we might wonder in what respects Milton's would have been different if he had never married at all.

In a more general way Saurat's overemphasis on biography and sex leads him to distort the nature of

the temptation and of Milton's main theme. The poet
being what Saurat says he is, the temptation has to turn
on Adam's succumbing to sensual passion. It is true
that Adam sins against the dictates of religion and
reason because his love for Eve oversways his will; but
that is the essence of the traditional conception of the
fall. On the other hand, Saurat neglects the far more
elaborate treatment of the temptation of Eve. If we
read the poem with our own eyes, we can hardly miss
Milton's continual stress on the motive of irreligious
intellectual pride as opposed to religious humility.
Satan, who himself had fallen through pride, decides
to base his campaign on that; he will appeal to the ambitious craving for godlike knowledge. This is the motive of the dream he puts into Eve's mind, of his successful dialogue with her, of her soliloquies before and
after her sin, and of her persuasion of Adam. It is the
moral of Raphael's long discourse on astronomy, and it
is strongly reiterated in the most significant place, the
conclusion of the poem, where religious faith and love
and obedience are contrasted with merely scientific
and external knowledge. All this, a large part of Milton's central theme, Saurat passes by; such "obscurant-
ism" is of course incompatible with his view of Milton
the man and the thinker. Like too many critics, Saurat
does not take sufficient account of the effect upon Milton of advancing age, disillusionizing experience, and
deepening religious insight; for him the author of
Paradise Lost is still the bold pamphleteer. So too,
when Christ in *Paradise Regained* breaks out against
vain bookishness, Saurat cannot square the utterance

with his notion of the great heretical rationalist and has to find an explanation, a rather feeble one, in the poet's fatigue.

If, in this short paper, Saurat is given a kind of bad eminence, it is an indirect and partial acknowledgment of the stimulating value of his work. We could glance at many other examples, old and new, of the use of biographical evidence and find similar mixtures of sound and unsound results; but everyone can supply such examples for himself and I need not assemble a list. When, to sum up, we review a good deal of Miltonic criticism, scholarly as well as unscholarly, from Johnson to Saurat and Eliot, we may arrive at the tentative conclusion that biographical evidence *is* of the first importance for the study of Milton—that is, that we need to look into the biographies of his critics.

To come to the general aspects of the problem, I may say at once that I have no special revelation. I can offer only a small set of truisms. It may, I should think, be laid down as a theoretical axiom that, if a work of art is not a self-sufficient entity and does not make its essential impact without biographical aids, there is something wrong with it (unless, of course, it has a topical subject). Nobody, we may remember, knows more than a few meager facts about most of the Greek and Roman writers, but we do not for that reason assume that we are debarred from comprehending ancient literature. And if our general axiom holds (with some reservations to be noted in a moment), it ought to be especially true of Milton, who is recognized by friend and foe alike as the classical artist *par excel-*

lence in English poetry. The word "classical," to be sure, embraces a number of qualities, but near the center are impersonality and normality.

For the reservations, it is understood that our theoretical reader is capable of bringing the author's other writings, prose as well as verse, to bear upon a particular poem. Also, it is freely granted that biographical evidence, though not a direct factor in the aesthetic experience, may stimulate receptivity and thereby promote and enrich the experience. As I have said elsewhere, it is in itself a moving experience to follow and relive Milton's spiritual evolution, and any good teacher or critic will use biography, knowing, however, that the discussion of a poem as a document is a beginning and not an end. To make these last remarks is not, I think, to unsay the general axiom about a poem's self-sufficiency. If, theoretically, the fullest biographical knowledge is necessary for the comprehension of a poem, difficulties ensue. One large fact has been mentioned, our ignorance of Greek and Roman biography. In the present case, we should have to admit that only a handful of Milton specialists can understand Milton. Possibly we Milton specialists think so. But if we do, we must recognize that our undergraduate teaching of Milton is doomed to failure because of our students' meager knowledge, and, worse still, that we ourselves cannot understand the work of countless other authors of whose biographies we are not complete masters.

In other words, a poem of Milton's should yield pretty much its full significance to a reader who possesses a very few biographical facts. We might look at the greatest of the early poems, *Lycidas,* one of the supreme examples in all English poetry of impersonal art charged with personal emotion. Although Milton had no such reason as Tennyson to feel personal sorrow, and although his own past, present, and future are his theme, he is asking himself the question of *In Memoriam*: how can he believe in God's providential care of a world in which a virtuous and promising life is cut off, a life, moreover, dedicated to the church which God allows to be infested with hireling shepherds? The pastoral convention provides a dramatic mask and controlling pattern for the poet's surging emotions, and beneath the smooth surface the struggle with doubt goes on until it ends with religious affirmation and serenity. If we see and feel this struggle and resolution as we should, how much of our response, we may ask, depends upon biographical knowledge gained outside the poem? Is there anything except two facts, and supplementary facts at that— namely, that the poet had recoiled bitterly from the church for which he had been destined, and that he wrote the poem after five long years of hard and outwardly unprofitable study? Everything else, except a modicum of literary and historical knowledge, is given in the poem. Further, since there have been some intelligent readers who could see in *Lycidas* nothing but an academic exercise, we might ask what would be the remedy for them, saturation in biography or saturation in the poem?

Let us move on to what may be called the *Lycidas* of Milton's old age, *Samson Agonistes,* which constitutes the most obvious test case. We are all—except Mr. Leavis—aware that *Samson* is the one great drama in English on the Greek model, that it is packed with intense emotion of a more profound and complex kind than inspired *Lycidas*. The theme is the process of Samson's regeneration, his development, under successive temptations, away from self-centered pride and despair to selfless humility and renewed trust in God. For most readers, perhaps, the drama is the most completely alive of all Milton's major works. That is, its original aim and effect are communicated the most fully, with the least loss through altered times and ideas, the least necessity for historical and philosophical reconstructions. Like the dramas of Aeschylus and Sophocles, it poses a universal and timeless problem in universal terms.

At the same time, as everyone knows, it can be read as an intensely personal document. With our knowledge, we see Restoration England and John Milton in the whole picture of Israel subject to a godless race and of the great rebel and deliverer now blind, helpless, tortured by physical and mental pains, while the bodies of other leaders are a prey to dogs and fowls, unjust tribunals, and the ungrateful mob; in the condemnation of the oppressors' idolatry, levity, and *hybris;* and, some would say, in the hero's fatal marriage to a daughter of the enemy—since the ghost of Mary Powell gets around much more surprisingly than that of Hamlet's father.

But one cannot bring up this familiar parallelism without adding some equally obvious comments. One is that even in his grand testament Milton remains a classical artist who depersonalizes and generalizes his public and private emotions. Every single item that we can call personal is an essential item in the drama of the Hebrew hero and arouses the appropriate dramatic reaction. Further, if we ask what the early biographers tell us, we find pictures of a man who, despite gout and blindness and other troubles, enjoys a placid and cheerful old age, with music, books, meditation, and the company that his character and fame have drawn about him. The biographies do not in any real sense explain either the old poet's capacity for defiance of the Restoration government or his much-tried but invincible religious faith. What we know of the state of mind that gave birth to *Samson* we infer from his verse and his pre-Restoration prose. Finally, if what we infer about Milton's personal experience and outlook explains the bare fact that he was able to bring emotional exaltation and intensity to the story of Samson, it is not "autobiography" that chiefly affects us. If the drama did not in itself move us greatly, our biographical knowledge would not bring it to life. When we respond as we do to "Eyeless in Gaza at the Mill with slaves," is it because we are thinking of Milton himself? Suppose, for instance, that we could work out parallels between the experience of Aeschylus and that of Prometheus: would such parallels appreciably heighten our response to the Greek drama?

We have only touched on some central questions concerning *Lycidas, Paradise Lost,* and *Samson,* but if we had time to look at all of Milton's poems I think we should find that their effect does not depend upon biographical information. From beginning to end, Milton's "self-expression" was objectified, generalized, and controlled by the dynamic principle of "decorum." Even in what appear to be the directly personal invocations of *Paradise Lost*, as C. S. Lewis has remarked, Milton is not speaking as a particular individual but is rather dramatizing himself as "the Christian poet" or "the blind poet." It is clearly essential to our full appreciation of the early poems that we should know something of the young idealist's situation and temper. It is also essential to our full appreciation of the major poems that we should realize what has happened to the young idealist, what these late works represent in their author's spiritual evolution: that the militant and confident revolutionist has lost his faith in mass movements, that he has been driven back to his impregnable inner fortress, that he has learned upon his pulses that "In His will is our peace." But all the essential knowledge we get from the works themselves, with help from Milton's other writings, not from biography. If we simply read *Paradise Lost* without prepossessions, its central import is fairly plain. Of course the more we know of literature, philosophy, and theology, the fuller our understanding, but that is a different affair—and the use of that kind of evidence and illustration, like the use of biography, can yield biased results. Even our glance at *Paradise Lost*, which is of course the crux of Miltonic interpretation, would suggest that critical deficiencies and aberrations have been largely caused by the use of biographical evidence. The critic's conscious or unconscious endeavor has often been not to study the poem itself, but to fit the poem into his picture of the man; hence the distortions in regard to rebellious pride, sensuality, Puritanism, and what not. We might conclude, then, that biographical evidence, as commonly used, has been as much of a hindrance as a help; but that, in the hands of ideally tactful and judicious scholar-critics (such as you and I), it can and should be useful in recreating the circumstances of composition, in promoting a receptive attitude, and perhaps now and then in throwing light on the text. Since Milton's poetry has suffered not only from recent prejudices in poetical taste but from prejudice against the man, the Miltonic scholar may well consider it part of his mission to establish a right view of the man. But that, however desirable, is only wiping spots off the spectacles with which we read the poetry.[3]

[3] While reading the proof of this paper I received from a student in my Milton course an amiable letter in which he said that he was left, above all, "with an appreciation of Milton as a human being, a fact which seems to me to be vital to an understanding of his work." This intelligent young Miltonist's emphasis made me wonder if there is a discrepancy between my preaching and my practice; but possibly it is covered by the reservations made in the paper.

Jonathan Swift

❧

By LOUIS A. LANDA

IT IS RARE INDEED that a commentator appraises any
work of Jonathan Swift without reference to biographical fact. If one of Swift's minor efforts is under
discussion, as the poem "The Lady's Dressing Room,"
we may expect the critical judgment to rest upon some
such basis as that presented by Sir Walter Scott, who
wished the poem to be interpreted in the light of the
author's peculiar habits and state of mind. If Part III
of *Gulliver's Travels,* where Swift attacks the corruptions of learning, is the object of consideration, the
commentator is certain to make an excursion back to
Swift's student days at Trinity College, Dublin, to explain that here began his life-long hatred of science and
philosophy. And so with the other works, to the point
that the criticism of Swift is a sustained endeavor to interpret the writings in the light of the man, although
anyone who reads the critics of Swift will be aware too
of a simultaneous and converse process—attempts to
interpret the man in the light of the works.

With respect to Swift we are often confronted not

only with the critical significance of biographical evidence but as well with the biographical significance of critical evidence. It is easy to find commentators who will have it both ways, commentators, for example, who assume a morbid state of mind in Swift as an explanation of his scatalogical verse, then use the scatalogical verse to prove that the author undoubtedly was morbid. Traditionally the criticism of Swift's works is so inextricably mingled with biography that one looks almost in vain for critical judgments based upon merely aesthetic assumptions.

The persistent tendency of the commentators has been to assume a direct and fairly simple reflection in the works of the nature and personality of Swift; and such a work as *Gulliver's Travels* has as often as not been viewed as both a strange and puzzling psychological case history and a representation of its author's objective experiences. No one can doubt for a moment the validity and the fruitfulness of the biographical approach to *Gulliver's Travels* in particular or to Swift's works in general. Considering the character of his writings—their personal, intimate, and topical nature—this approach is the natural one. Yet I think that the interpretation of Swift has at times suffered somewhat from this tendency, this unwillingness of the commentator to detach the work from the man. But the overemphasis upon this approach is rather less disturbing than its misapplication or its loose and incautious use. Commentators who would doubtless feel some hesitation in equating Fielding with Tom Jones or Sterne with Tristram Shandy can accept with ap-

parent ease as a premise of their criticism that Swift is
Gulliver. In what follows I wish, first of all, to comment on certain recurring biographical considerations
which have played a part—a not very happy part—in
the criticism of Swift's works for a period of two centuries, and, secondly, to present some instances in
which other biographical considerations of value for
criticism have not been explored sufficiently.

The problem which has most preoccupied Swift's
critics has been the pessimism and misanthropy of
Gulliver's Travels and the endeavor to explain these
qualities in the work by searching for exactly cor-
responding qualities in Swift himself. Part IV of *Gulliver's Travels,* with its contrasting picture of Yahoo
and Houyhnhnm, has been the focal point of the discussions, and ordinarily the commentators have acted
on the assumption, though not always consciously,
that here in Part IV is the real key to Swift. It is maintained or implied that in Part IV are the possibilities of
a final comprehension and the basis of a final judgment. The image of Swift—the rather horrendous
image—which has been transmitted from generation
to generation is chiefly the image deduced from Part
IV, enforced by a careful selection of biographical
fact or myth appropriately chosen to stress the severe
lineaments of his character. Only occasionally is the
image, a monochrome, softened by reference to the
playful Swift, to Swift the author of delightful light
verse, the punster, the genial companion of Queen
Anne's Lord Treasurer and her Secretary of State, or to
the Swift who was a charming guest at great houses and

who had a genius for friendship among both sexes.

Perhaps for purposes of discussion we may ignore the volume and range of Swift's works and grant the unwarranted assumption that the masterpiece is somehow the man, and that a particular portion of the masterpiece—Part IV of *Gulliver*—is of such fundamental significance as to outweigh various other considerations. If we trace the progress of the criticism of *Gulliver's Travels* from Swift's earliest biographer, the Earl of Orrery, to the twentieth century, we find preponderantly and repetitiously a set of severe judgments passed on Part IV, judgments referable back to Swift the man. In his *Remarks on the Life and Writings of Dr. Jonathan Swift* (1752), Orrery climaxes his comment with the statement that "no man [was] better acquainted [than Swift] with human nature, both in the highest, and in the lowest scenes of life" (p. 338). Yet, contradictorily, in discussing Part IV of *Gulliver* he observes that Swift's misanthropy is "intolerable," adding that "the representation which he has given us of human nature, must terrify, and even debase the mind of the reader who views it" (p. 184). Orrery then proceeds to a lengthy vindication of mankind mingled with violent charges against Swift, among them that in painting the Yahoos Swift became one himself and that the "voyage to the Houyhnhnms is a real insult upon mankind" (p. 190). Orrery is significant because with few exceptions his is the tone and pretty much the method of criticism of the Fourth Voyage for a century and a half. The fundamental points raised are concerned with the motives or the personality of the author who would present this particular conception of human nature; and Orrery's explanation of Part IV in terms of injured pride, personal disappointments, and a soured temper becomes as time goes on the traditional one.

Even an occasional defender of Swift, as his good friend Patrick Delany, who answers Orrery point by point, is unwilling to undertake the defense of the last book of *Gulliver;* and he too lets fall such phrases as "moral deformity" and "defiled imagination." The eighteenth-century commentators, taking a high moral line, maintained that Swift's misanthropy had led him to write, as James Beattie phrased it, "a monstrous fiction." It was variously and characteristically stated: the gloomy and perverse Dean had talents that tended toward the wicked rather than the sublime; he was motivated by a malignant wish to degrade and brutalize the human race; he had written a libel on human nature. Though generally these commentators prefer to denounce the moral aspects of the Voyage to Houyhnhnmland and the degraded nature of the author, they leave no doubt that they think Part IV an artistic failure as well. In their eyes moral culpability and artistic failure have a necessary connection. The premise seems to be that a person of unsound views concerning human nature or of false moral views cannot write an artistically sound work. It is as though a Buddhist should deny literary value to Dante's *Divine Comedy* or Milton's *Paradise Lost* because these works are ethically and religiously unsound.

Yet it ought to be said to the honor of the eighteenth-century commentators that they generally paid the author of *Gulliver* the compliment of believing him a sane man. It remained for certain nineteenth-century critics to take a new tack and to elaborate a less defensible charge. Though they accepted the view that the Fourth Voyage could be explained in terms of a depraved author, they *added* that it might well be explained in terms of a mad author. The charge of madness was usually presented with a certain caution. Two commentators in the middle of the century may be taken as examples of the willingness to accuse Swift of insanity and the unwillingness, at the same time, to come out unreservedly. In the *North British Review* of 1849 a reviewer writes of Swift's work that it is *"more or less* symptomatic of mental disease" (italics mine); and in the following year, in the London *Times,* a writer says that Swift was "more or less mad." It is possible that Sir Walter Scott is responsible for this wavering between outright and qualified assertion. In his edition of Swift's *Works* (1814) he writes that we cannot justify, by saying that it has a moral purpose, "the nakedness with which Swift has sketched this horrible outline of mankind degraded to a bestial state" (1883 ed., I, 315). He prefers to explain the misanthropy of *Gulliver* as the result of "the *first* impressions of . . . *incipient* mental disease" (italics mine). There are nineteenth-century commentators who felt that the Fourth Voyage should not be read. Thackeray gave such advice to the audience who listened to his lectures on the English humorists of the eighteenth century in 1851; and, later, Edmund Gosse—using such phrases as "the horrible satisfaction of disease" and a brain "not wholly under control"—declared that the "horrible foulness of this satire on the Yahoo . . . banishes from decent households a fourth part of one of the most brilliant and delightful of English books." It is somewhat more surprising to find W. E. H. Lecky, who usually showed a well-balanced and sympathetic understanding of Swift, falling into the jargon. He can see Swift's misanthropy as a constitutional melancholy "mainly due to a physical malady which had long acted upon his brain." [1] It is not surprising, however, that in the twentieth century the psychoanalysts have seized on so attractive a subject as Swift; and now we find *Gulliver* explained in terms of neuroses and complexes. The following quotation is taken from the *Psychoanalytic Review* of 1942: *Gulliver's Travels* "may be viewed as a neurotic phantasy with coprophilia as its main content." It furnishes

abundant evidence of the neurotic makeup of the author and discloses in him a number of perverse trends indicative of fixation at the anal sadistic stage of libidinal development. Most conspicuous among those perverse trends is that of coprophilia, although the work furnishes evidence of numerous other related neurotic characteristics accompanying the general picture of psychosexual infantilism and emotional immaturity.

By a diligent search this psychoanalyst was able to discover in *Gulliver's Travels* strains of misogyny, misanthropy, mysophilia, mysophobia, voyeurism, exhibitionism, and compensatory potency reactions. If

[1] Introduction to the *Prose Works of Jonathan Swift*, ed. T. Scott, 1897, I, lxxxviii.

this psychoanalytic approach seems to have in it an element of absurdity, we should recognize that it is only a logical development of the disordered-intellect theory of the nineteenth-century critics, the chief difference being that the terminology has changed and that the psychoanalyst frankly sees *Gulliver's Travels* as case history, whereas the critics were presumably making a literary appraisal. Perhaps these crude and amateur attempts deserve little attention, yet they are a phenomenon that the serious student of Swift can hardly ignore in the light of their recurrence and their effectiveness in perpetuating myths. And they sometimes come with great persuasiveness and literary flavor, as witness Mr. Aldous Huxley's essay in which, by virtue of ignoring nine tenths of Swift's works, he can arrive at an amazingly oversimplified explanation of Swift's greatness: "Swift's greatness," Mr. Huxley writes, "lies in the intensity, the almost insane violence, of that 'hatred of bowels' which is the essence of his misanthropy and which underlies the whole of his work" (*Do What You Will*, 1930, p. 105).

I suggest that the commentators who have relied on a theory of insanity or disordered intellect to explain Swift's works have weakened their case, if they have not vitiated it entirely, by resorting to ex post facto reasoning. The failure of Swift's mental faculties toward the end of his life—some fifteen or sixteen years after the publication of *Gulliver's Travels*—was seized upon to explain something the critics did not like and frequently did not understand. It seemed to them valid to push his insanity back in time, to look retrospectively at the intolerable fourth book of *Gulliver's Travels,* and to infer that Swift's insanity must have been at least incipient when he wrote it. One recent commentator, rather more zealous than others, hints that the madness can be traced as far back as *A Tale of a Tub.* Commentators who observe manifestations of a disordered intellect in the Fourth Voyage have not thought to question the intellect behind the Third Voyage, yet we know now that the third was composed in point of time after the fourth. And these commentators have nothing but praise for the vigor, the keenness, the sanity, and the humanity of the mind that produced the *Drapier's Letters,* yet we have reasonable assurance that Swift completed the draft of Part IV of *Gulliver* in January of 1724 and was at work on the first of the *Drapier's Letters* in February.

Another procedure of which the critics of Swift are fond deserves to be scanned: the habit of taking an isolated statement or an isolated incident and giving it undue significance to support their prepossessions. In a recent study of Swift, in many respects of more than ordinary perceptiveness, the author considers Part IV of *Gulliver* as an embodiment of the tragic view of life. In so doing he passes from the work to the facts or presumed facts of Swift's life to enforce his interpretation, adducing as evidence the report of Swift's manner, in his later years, of bidding friends good-by: "Good night, I hope I shall never see you again." If Swift really used this remark, if he used it seriously, some weight may be attached to it; but I should want to know to whom he used it and in what tone or spirit.

It sounds very much like his usual banter, his manner of friendly insult and quite genial vituperation which so often distinguishes his letters to friends who understood his ironic turn and his liking for the inverted compliment. How can we rely on such casual remarks or possibly know what weight to give them? But such a remark is related to Swift's habit of reading certain parts of the Book of Job to prove that he hated life, and is made to seem of a piece with the Fourth Voyage of *Gulliver's Travels*. This is typical of the commentators who have culled from Swift's letters, from the biographies, and from other documents all the presumed evidence of gloom and misanthropy in order to uncover what they have a strong prepossession to uncover, the essential misery of his existence. This is the way to prove, in support of the interpretation of the Fourth Voyage, that "Swift's life was a long disease, with its disappointments, its self-torture, its morbid recriminations."

But a matter of statistical balance is involved here: the facts listed and weighted heavily have been too much of one complexion. Too much has been made of the last years of Swift's life, when he bothered less to conceal his moods and his irritations—and when he seemed to get a certain satisfaction in talking about his ailments. I should like to see some biographer counter the gloomy approach by emphasizing Swift's zest for life, his vitality, and the playfulness of his mind. There is ample evidence in his letters—and in what we know of his activities—of high spirits, good humor, and daily satisfactions. Such a study might very well, without distortion, evidence an unexpected mathematical balance between happiness and unhappiness.

I should not want to be put into the position of denying Swift a considerable pessimism and a fair share of misanthropy. These qualities, however, were not so raw or so unassimilated or so crudely operative in his daily existence as has been often represented. The manner in which these personal qualities have been used to explain *Gulliver* deserves to be questioned. It has been an overly simple process of equating biographical fact and artistic statement, of viewing the work as a transcription of the author's experiences or as a precise and complete representation of his personal philosophy—or as a final explanation of his personality. There is an obvious danger in seeing an artistic or imaginative construction as mere duplication. *Gulliver's Travels* is a work of mingled fantasy and satire; it is Utopian literature, highly allusive and symbolic, charged with hidden meanings and projected to a level several removes from the real world of its author.

To leaven the biographical approach other questions deserve attention. What are the artistic necessities of a work of this type? What are the aesthetic principles, quite apart from other considerations, that shape the work? To what extent is there a compromise between these principles and the conscious or the undeliberate tendency of the author to reflect his experiences and his personality?

If the biographical approach to Swift has been crudely used or overemphasized in certain respects,

there are other respects in which biographical considerations of critical value have been left almost
wholly unexplored. The most significant of these
seems to me to be Swift's profession as a Christian
divine. Is there in this some clue to an explanation of
Part IV of *Gulliver?* If a reading of the sermons can
be trusted, the eighteenth-century divine relished his
duty to expatiate on the evils and corruptions of this
world and the inadequacies of this life. He seemed to
enjoy measuring the imperfections before him against
a higher set of values. Swift, I think, would have held
an optimistic divine to be a contradiction in terms;
and his own pessimism is quite consonant with the pessimism at the heart of Christianity. One of Swift's sermons begins as follows:

The holy Scripture is full of expressions to set forth the
miserable condition of man during the whole progress of
his life; his weakness, pride, and vanity, his unmeasurable
desires, and perpetual disappointments; the prevalency of
his passions, and the corruptions of his reason, his delud-
ing hopes, and his real, as well as imaginary, fears . . .
his cares and anxieties, the diseases of his body, and the
diseases of his mind. . . . And the wise men of all ages
have made the same reflections.[2]

If Swift had written his own comment on *Gulliver's
Travels,* he might very well have used the words of
this sermon. *Gulliver's Travels* certainly is full of expressions to set forth the miserable condition of man—
his weakness, pride, and vanity, his unmeasurable desires, the prevalency of his passions and the corrup-

[2] *On The Poor Man's Contentment.*

tions of his reason—and so on through the catalogue. Indeed, Swift's few sermons and those of other eighteenth-century divines could easily be used to annotate *Gulliver's Travels*. It is difficult for me to believe that a contemporary could fail to see the affinity between the Fourth Voyage—or the whole of *Gulliver*—and many of the conventional sermons on human nature and the evils of this life. Swift's emphasis on depraved human nature and his evaluation of man's behavior are certainly *not* at odds with Christian tradition. There is no need to ascribe such views solely to personal bitterness or frustrations or melancholia. His thinking and status as a divine had an effect much more profound than is generally recognized. A good case can be made for Part IV of *Gulliver* as being in its implications Christian apologetics, though of course in nontheological terms; in a sense it is an allegory which veils human nature and society as a Christian divine views them. It is by indirection a defense of the doctrine of redemption and man's need of grace.

Only an occasional commentator has recognized and stressed the essentially Christian philosophy of the Fourth Voyage. The first was Swift's relative, Deane Swift, who declared that the Christian conception of the evil nature of man is the "groundwork of the whole satyre contained in the voyage to the Houyhnhnms." Then this cousin of Jonathan Swift, this lesser Swift, delivers himself of a catalogue of vices worthy of his great cousin:

Ought a preacher of righteousness [he asks], ought a watch-
man of the Christian faith . . . to hold his peace . . .
when avarice, fraud, cheating, violence, rapine, extortion,
cruelty, oppression, tyranny, rancour, envy, malice, detrac-
tion, hatred, revenge, murder, whoredom, adultery, lasciv-
iousness, bribery, corruption, pimping, lying, perjury,
subornation, treachery, ingratitude, gaming, flattery,
drunkenness, gluttony, luxury, vanity, effeminacy, cow-
ardice, pride, impudence, hypocrisy, infidelity, blasphemy,
idolatry, sodomy, and innumerable other vices are as
epidemical as the pox, and many of them the notorious
characteristicks of the bulk of mankind? [3]

"Dr. Swift," he adds, "was not the first preacher,
whose writings import this kind of philosophy." Surely
those clergymen who week after week exposed the
deceitfulness of the human heart would have agreed
with Deane Swift.

It seems to be true, as T. O. Wedel has pointed out,[4]
that Swift's view of human nature was opposed to certain contemporary attitudes in which the passions of
men were looked on kindly and in which the dignity
of human nature was defended in such a way that the
doctrine of original sin lost its efficacy. In his *Reason-
ableness of Christianity* (1695) John Locke could deny,
without raising much serious protest, that the fall of
Adam implies the corruption of human nature in
Adam's posterity. It is this same current of thought

[3] *Essay upon the Life, Writings, and Character of Dr. Swift* (1755),
pp. 219–20.
[4] For the relationship between Swift and Wesley stated in this paragraph see an article to which I am much indebted, T. O. Wedel, "On
the Philosophical Background of *Gulliver's Travels,*" *Studies in Philology*, XXIII (1926), 434–50.

that later in the century disturbed John Wesley, who complains in one of his sermons (No. XXXVIII, "Original Sin") that "not a few persons of strong understanding, as well as extensive learning, have employed their utmost abilities to show, what they termed, 'the fair side of human nature in Adam's posterity.' " "So that," Wesley continues, "it is now quite unfashionable to say anything to the disparagement of human nature; which is generally allowed, notwithstanding a few infirmities, to be very innocent, and wise, and virtuous." Is it not significant, when Wesley comes to write his treatise on *The Doctrine of Original Sin* (1756), that he should turn to Swift, to Part IV of *Gulliver* for quotations? In this treatise Wesley refers scornfully to those "who gravely talk of the dignity of our nature," and then quotes several times from what he calls "a late eminent hand." The "late eminent hand" is Swift's, whose words from Part IV of *Gulliver* describing man as "a lump of deformity and disease, both in body and mind, smitten with pride" Wesley has seized on. Wesley refers again and again to the "many laboured panegyrics . . . we now read and hear on the dignity of human nature"; and he raises a question which is, I think, a clue to Swift. If men are generally virtuous, what is the need of the doctrine of Redemption? This is pretty much the point of two sermons by Swift, where he is obviously in reaction to the panegyrics on human nature which came from Shaftesbury and the benevolists, from the defenders of the Stoic wise man, and from proponents of the concept of a man of honor. Swift sensed the

danger to orthodox Christianity from an ethical system or any view of human nature stressing man's
goodness or strongly asserting man's capacity for virtue. He had no faith in the existence of the benevolent
man of Shaftesbury and the anti-Hobbists, the proud,
magnanimous man of the Stoics, or the rational man of
the deists; his man is a creature of the passions, of pride
and self-love, a frail and sinful being in need of redemption. The very simple and wholly unoriginal
strain of apologetics in Swift's sermons is based upon
an attitude common in traditional Christian thought;
and to my way of thinking Swift the clergyman repeats
himself in *Gulliver's Travels.*

It might be of value to carry the consideration of
Swift the clergyman beyond application to *Gulliver,* to
discover whether his activities in his profession may
not throw some light on his other works—the Irish
tracts, for example. Those who make a case for Swift's
misanthropy, his pessimism and gloom, his tragic view
of life, can point to these tracts to enforce their views.
Can we accept the Irish tracts as "monuments to
despair, pessimism, bitterness, hopelessness and hate;
and like his other works . . . distillations of the
man"? It is certainly true that the tracts reflect disil-
lusionment, and are filled with statements that reflect hopelessness. Undoubtedly they are charged with
bitterness; yet it is not necessarily the bitterness of a
man who hates his fellow men or thinks them not
worth saving. The real note is perhaps despair, despair
at corruption and weakness; but it is obvious that
Swift's *words* of despair were tempered by hope that

something might be achieved to relieve the Irish people. Until the end of his active life he persisted in writing and working to achieve reforms. His continued zest for reform is significant, even though he assures us frequently that he is without hope. He did not withdraw to nurse his bitterness or his misanthropy. Is it not conceivable that the tone, the emotional coloring, the violent rhetoric of the Irish tracts are susceptible to an explanation in terms other than personal bitterness or pessimism? Are not the rhetorical qualities, the strong expressions, appropriate to the purpose in hand and proper from a clergyman and reformer bent on seeing maladjustments corrected? Swift's occupation, his position as dean and dignitary, gave him the opportunity and imposed on him the obligation to take cognizance of private and public distresses. He dispensed the Cathedral funds for private and public benefactions; he sat on numerous charity commissions; he was requested and expected to make his views known on public ills. As a dignitary in a hapless country, it was—to say the least—mathematically probable that he should encounter conditions to call forth gloomy expressions. If a sensitive, public-spirited, socially conscious Irishman of Swift's day were anything but gloomy, then indeed we would need an explanation. Irish conditions being what they were, Swift's lamentations, the fierce and desperate rhetoric, are a natural product of a man doing his duty in an appropriately chosen diction. It was Swift's job to spy out the worst and to call attention to it in the strongest language he could command. By his calling he was a specialist in disorders; and here we have possibly a sufficient explanation of the tone of the Irish tracts without recourse to any theory of personality or misanthropy.

The Irish tracts, including the *Drapier's Letters,* offer another instance of the way in which interpretation and biographical considerations enforce each other—and at the same time a further instance of how easily divergent views may be arrived at. If a person without any knowledge of Swift came to the tracts without prepossessions, he would carry away with him, despite certain qualifications, the general impression of an Irish patriot moved by a genuine desire for the national welfare. Swift would obviously appear to be concerned to protect Ireland from exploitation at the hands of a powerful England. There is, certainly, a note of scorn for the slothful and dirty native Irish; but there is also a note of strong compassion and a tendency to absolve them from blame in the light of intolerable conditions which they could hardly be expected to transcend. In a letter of 1732 he writes that the English ought to be "ashamed of the reproaches they cast on the ignorance, the dulness, and the want of courage, in the Irish natives; those defects . . . arising only from the poverty and slavery they suffer from their inhuman neighbors . . . the millions of oppressions they lie under . . . have been enough to damp the best spirits under the sun." [5] It is not accidental that the English authorities viewed Swift as dangerous, and certain of his tracts as openly inciting

[5] *Correspondence,* ed. E. Ball (1910–14), IV, 328.

the Irish to make themselves independent of England. Indeed his sense of Ireland's rights as a nation to develop its own economy and to control its own destiny is at times so vigorously expressed—his words probably go beyond his intention—that he can easily be taken as a confirmed nationalist.

And thus the Irish claim Swift as the Hibernian Patriot. In 1782, when Grattan secured the adoption of the declaration of Irish independence in the Irish House of Commons, he took the floor to apostrophize Swift (and Molyneux) in these words: "Spirit of Swift! Your genius has prevailed. Ireland is now a nation!" This view of Swift as the "first and greatest of Irish nationalists" found stronger and stronger proponents as time went on. In the last part of the nineteenth century we find this not uncharacteristic utterance: "No one can now talk of Irish liberty, the Irish nation, Irish manufactures, Irish grievances, and Irish rights without speaking the language and echoing the thoughts of Swift. When [he] denounced Wood's Halfpence he was not thinking at all of finance and currency. He was after quite other game. He meant to build up an Irish nation." In the twentieth century such enthusiasm eventuates in the view, recently propounded, that Swift's sympathies were with the silent and hidden Ireland rather than with the Protestant Ascendancy and that the native Irish "made him a God of their Gaelic Olympus, and even imagined that he was secretly of their faith." A year does not pass without discussion in some Irish journal of the exact nature of Swift's Irishism.

Yet there is the other side, equally well supported by biographical materials. Certain fierce defenders of Irish nationalism will have none of Swift. Admitting that some of his efforts had good results, they still insist that the facts of Swift's biography leave no interpretation possible but that Swift was an Englishman of the hated Protestant Ascendancy. The Irish nation was for him the English Pale. Catholic and Celtic Ireland hardly existed for him. It has been pointed out that in Swift's day the Gaels had hundreds of poets to express their feelings and that these poets were often politically self-conscious; yet in their works are no references to the Dean or the Drapier.

The case is strengthened by a careful selection of biographical fact: Swift's insistence that his birth in Ireland was mere accident; his pride in his Yorkshire ancestry; his desire for residence and a career in England; and his reference to his being exiled in Ireland; his resistance to any attempt to spread the use of the Irish language. But what weighs most heavily with the proponents of this view is that Swift had, they insist, no real concern for Catholic Ireland, that he favored the harsh penal laws against the Catholics, and that his concern was only for the Anglo-Irish Anglicans. As usual, Swift's words and actions are interpreted with considerable asperity, and he is seen as defending Ireland less out of humanity than out of a desire to revenge himself on his enemy, Robert Walpole and the Whig administration in England. This is the familiar Swift—and the familiar application of his biography to interpretation—Swift, the man of violent personal prejudices, moved by envy and disappointed ambition, whose every act, known or surmised, whose every utterance, public or private, and whose person- ality in every facet, real or imagined, are brought to bear in the interpretation of his works.

Shelley's Ferrarese Maniac

✹

By CARLOS BAKER

THE BUSINESS of fixing exactly the critical significance of the biographical evidence is one of the
most vexatious problems in Shelley criticism. It is
vexatious because in both critical and biographical
books on Shelley there has existed from the first a
strong inclination towards the autobiographical interpretation of much of the poetry. Other interpretations
have been tried. Yet even where they have been tried,
the ghost of autobiography is likely to rise in the midst
of the argument and shake its chains.

The autobiographical interpretation of Shelley's
poems, if judiciously used, can be of real, though an-
cillary, value. But it is the thesis of the present essay
that the sporadic but persistent tendency towards the
autobiographical interpretation of many of the poems
has acted as a serious obstacle to the better understanding of some of the things Shelley was trying to do,
and the methods by which he achieved his purpose.
The aim will be to begin by enumerating some of the
reasons for the interest in Shelleyan biography, and

then to examine in detail a particular problem—that offered by *Julian and Maddalo*—in the hope that such a detailed examination will serve both to support and to illustrate the thesis.

From a considerably longer list of possibilities, one may mention four reasons for the continued stress on autobiography in the interpretation of Shelley's poems. The first is that Mary's notes in her collected editions of the poetry are mainly biographical. This in itself is nothing to deplore. It is not often that a writer leaves a widow so intelligent, so skilled in rhetoric, and so well informed about the circumstances under which many of the poems were written, and there would be many more gaps in the available knowledge about Shelley if Mary's work had not been done. The influence of her notes among subsequent editors has been, of course, pervasive. But the blessing is mixed, for Mary had neither so subtle a mind, so lively an imagination, nor so much literary learning as her husband. She is sometimes in the right church without being in the right pew, and she is likely to stress biography, which she knew about, and to under-emphasize literary influences of which she was imperfectly aware.

Another reason for the stress on autobiography is that the chroniclers of Shelley's life have often disagreed both as to the facts, and the interpretation of the facts. These disagreements, while generating a certain amount of light, have also produced every degree of heat. Among Shelley's contemporary biographers, Hogg, Peacock, Medwin, and Trelawny, disagreements were frequent. In the Victorian period, writers of such varying mentalities as J. C. Jeaffreson, Mark Twain, and Matthew Arnold ranged themselves for a variety of reasons against Edward Dowden and Lady Jane Shelley. In our own day, Professors John Harrington Smith and Robert Metcalf Smith have already disagreed with some aspects of Professor White's definitive biography of Shelley,[1] while lengthy replies to Professor Robert Smith's highly controversial publication, *The Shelley Legend,* have been published by Professor White and Professor F. L. Jones, the editor of Mary Shelley's letters.[2] The persistent quarrels over Shelley's relations with women—whether there was any justification for the desertion of Harriet, whether Shelley was involved in sexual relations with Claire Clairmont and Emilia Viviani, whether he was the real or only the foster father of his Neapolitan ward, and whether the coldness which arose between Shelley and Mary in 1819 had anything to do with sexual jealousy—these are all quarrels and questions in the pyrotechnic class. Controversies over these questions have set biographers to searching the poems for possible telling details, some very tenuous arguments have been broached,[3] and the total effect has been to lay

[1] John Harrington Smith, "Shelley and Claire Again," *Studies in Philology,* XLI (1944), 94–105. R. M. Smith, Theodore G. Ehrsam, and others, *The Shelley Legend* (New York, 1945), *passim.*

[2] Newman I. White, *"The Shelley Legend* Examined," *Studies in Philology,* XLIII (1946), 522–44; F. L. Jones, *PMLA,* LXI (1946), 848–90.

[3] In the class of tenuous arguments would fall J. H. Smith's ridiculous suggestion that Shelley, Byron, and Claire Clairmont appear under thin disguises in *The Revolt of Islam.* "Laon and the bru-

undue stress on the autobiographical interpretation of some of the poems.

One or two general remarks on the current controversy are pertinent to the present purpose. Professor Smith's *Shelley Legend* is a vigorous, aggressive, and (according to Professors White and Jones) a very wrong-headed book. It contains certain factual errors, and certain half-truths. Even though these aspects of the book are unfortunate, one may still believe that in the world of democratic scholarship it is desirable that minorities rise up from time to time to challenge the position of a majority of Shelley scholars. The very fact that Professor White's *Shelley* is so nearly definitive a biography, the very fact that it is so exhaustive, so generally sound, so persuasively written, and so intentionally honest in every way, requires that some of White's positions be challenged. For a biography as good as White's is so rare that it immediately becomes a primary and therefore widely influential reference work for Shelley scholarship. But to say that the book is in the main trustworthy is not to say that Professor White—or any man of comparable scholarly stature— can do no wrong. It is rather to say that he does so little wrong, as one checks and doublechecks him against his source-documents, that the wrong he does do might seem to be of relatively little importance. When one is dealing with a widely influential reference work which is also a work of interpretation any wrong is of im-

---

nette Cythna are torn apart; during their period of separation Cythna is violated by the tyrant Othman (Lord Byron, I fear); she gives birth to a daughter" (*Studies in Philology*, XLI, 1944, 102).

portance. Therefore a challenge to the ruling party is both desirable and necessary.

Two more reasons for the continuing autobiographical stress in the reading of Shelley's poetry may be mentioned. Arnold's influential review of the Dowden biography played up a discrepancy he thought he saw between Shelley's life and his works. Arnold's conclusions about the life—that it was rather messy—and about the works—that they were charming and angelic—have both stuck like burrs to subsequent Shelleyans. Most of these have been more interested in proving that the life of Shelley was lived according to strict, though unorthodox, standards, and that it was therefore not messy but clean, than in showing that the poetry is something other than charming and angelic. Other neohumanist critics whose strong ethical bias is like Arnold's have evinced a decided dislike for what they felt to be Shelley's moral weakness, and have usually ended by agreeing with Arnold that a morally weak man can hardly be expected to have written morally strong poetry. This, of course, confronts Shelley's defenders with a dubious choice: they can either try to prove that Shelley was not morally weak, or they can try to prove that his poetry is morally strong. It is one of the interesting phenomena in Shelley scholarship that the poet's defenders have usually tried to prove that the poet was not morally weak, but only different from the common run of men. Where they have used the poetry to buttress their positions, they have nearly always used it for its autobiographical content.

Finally, it should be observed that the autobiographical emphasis is partly Shelley's own fault. He is
rather careless in distinguishing the ideal from the
real, probably because the two were not always completely distinguished in his own thinking. He also
displays a great love of mystification. He conceals his
real intentions in enigmatic utterances, and he does
not bother to explain some matters for which we
should very much like to have his own explanation.
Thus he concludes that strange gallimaufry of fact and
fiction, *Julian and Maddalo,* by having Julian, the
narrator, question Maddalo's daughter about the true
facts in the case of the Maniac. "She told me how all
happened," says Julian, "but the cold world shall not
know." The result is that there are a number of facts
about Shelley's poetry which the scholarly world,
whatever its temperature, has been unable to discover.

Although *Rosalind and Helen* was the first of Shelley's major poems to be brought to completion after
his arrival in Italy, the story of the life of Tasso was the
first subject to engage his attention. From Milan on the
sixth of April he wrote Peacock that he had been
meditating "many literary schemes, and one in particular," and that he wished to settle down somewhere
as quickly as possible in order to begin writing. The
particular scheme in his mind during April was a
verse tragedy on Tasso's madness and imprisonment, a
project never brought to completion.

In a villa at Este some six months later Shelley wrote,
either in whole or in part, the second of his people-

poems, *Julian and Maddalo,* and thereby inaugurated a mystery which has continued to puzzle Shelley critics ever since. A connection between the abortive Tasso drama and *Julian and Maddalo* has been twice suspected but unfortunately never proved. The crucial question has to do with the real identity of the Maniac whose complaint occupies a central position in the poem. Nobody has doubted, nor is there any reason to doubt, that the introductory portion of the poem is in the main an autobiographical account of Shelley's visit to Byron at Venice in August, 1818. The difficulty has been that an overwhelming majority of commentators have also wished to regard the story of the Maniac as autobiography, a position which raises the vexing question: To what extent does autobiography figure in this poem, and how far, for critical or biographical purposes, can allegedly autobiographical passages in Shelley be trusted?

Julian and Maddalo, although it can hardly be called a great poem, is a very useful document for the discussion of the critical significance of autobiographical evidence in Shelley. It is useful in that about one third of the poem is approximately true to autobiographical fact, that another third is true to what Shelley thought to be historical fact, and that the final third is demonstrably a piece of fiction.

The shape of the poem may be briefly indicated. Of the 617 lines, the first part, 211 lines, describes Shelley's actual visit to Byron at Venice on August 23–24, 1818. Shelley intended his friends to understand that Count Maddalo stood for Byron, and that Julian, the

English gentleman who pays the visit, represented himself. The poem opens with an account of Julian and Maddalo riding horseback along the sands of the Lido on an unseasonably cold day. This much is fact. By his own statement, Shelley called on Byron at three in the afternoon of Sunday, August 23, 1818, a cold day for that time of year. After some talk about Byron's illegitimate daughter, Allegra, the two men crossed to the Lido in Byron's gondola and rode horseback along the shore. Their conversation "consisted in the histories of [Byron's] wounded feelings, and questions [from Byron] as to [Shelley's] affairs." [4] They spoke of the Chancery decision which had deprived Shelley of his children by Harriet, and of "literary matters," specifically the fourth canto of *Childe Harold's Pilgrimage* and Leigh Hunt's *Foliage*. Then they returned to Byron's palace. The poem of course idealizes this encounter somewhat. The talk of Julian and Maddalo was first gay, then serious, Julian arguing against despondency, and Maddalo supporting the darker side.

From this point on the poem begins to diverge from the facts as they appear in Shelley's epistolary account of the visit.[5] One significant example of possible in-

[4] *Letters*, IX, 328. (*The Complete Works of Percy Bysshe Shelley*, ed. Ingpen and Peck, 10 vols.; Vol. IX: *Letters, 1812–1818*, ed. Ingpen, London and New York, 1926. Cited throughout as *Letters*, IX.)

[5] One minor example of this divergence may be found in the immediate aftermath of the ride. In the poem Julian is conveyed to his lodgings where he takes leave of Maddalo; in fact, Shelley returned to Byron's palace and seems to have spent most of the night talking with his host, since his letter describing the visit is dated five o'clock in the morning of Monday, August 24.

vention is the business about the island madhouse. On the way home from the Lido, Maddalo pointed out a madhouse on an island and made a passing remark about the inmates' being called to vespers. There is no assurance that this happened, although Byron and Shelley could probably have seen from their gondola either the madhouse on San Servolo or the penitentiary on San Clemente.[6] But Shelley's only demonstrable connection with prisons during his visit to Venice was the exploratory call he paid to the then empty dungeons of the Doges' Palace.[7]

There is a strong likelihood that Shelley invented most of the remainder of part one of *Julian and Maddalo* in order to ease his way into the lament of the Maniac. Julian goes the next morning to Maddalo's palace, plays for a little while with his host's small daughter, and, when the Count appears, resumes the talk of the preceding afternoon, preaching, as he then did, the necessity of aspiration.[8] Taking the other side

[6] W. E. Peck, *Shelley: His Life and Work* (Boston, 1927), II, 102, identifies the madhouse as that of San Servolo, although he notes Browning's statement that Shelley was probably confusing this madhouse with the penitentiary of San Clemente. See C. D. Locock, *Shelley's Poetical Works* (1911), I, 586. Medwin's statement that he had often seen the madhouse referred to in the poem may be of a piece with many of his other claims.

[7] *Letters*, IX, 335. According to Hobhouse, in his *Historical Illustrations of the Fourth Canto of Childe Harold* (1818), he and Byron had visited these same dungeons earlier in the same year. Byron may have suggested the visit to Shelley, but there is no evidence that he accompanied his friend to the Doges' Palace in August.

[8] Shelley may or may not have returned to Byron's palace Monday morning. He had been up rather late, and had business to attend to at "the Banker's." The playing at billiards with Count Maddalo's daughter sounds like something that might have taken place be-

as before, Maddalo proposes a visit to the island madhouse to which he had pointed the day before. There,
by listening to the wild talk of a particularly engaging
madman, Julian can learn more about the vanity of
human wishes.

The visit is undertaken, and the two friends ascend
to a well-furnished apartment where they have an
opportunity to observe the Maniac, a gentle and
pathetic creature who, in some mysterious fashion, has
been crossed in love, and who is engaged, by his own
account, in some kind of deception. As the visitors
listen, the Maniac delivers a lament of some 100 heroic
couplets. When he falls asleep, Julian returns to Maddalo's palace, dines there, and discusses the Maniac
with his host. Next morning he leaves Venice, and
many years elapse before his return. When he does
return, he asks Maddalo's now grown-up daughter
what happened to the Maniac. The young lady tells
him all the facts of the case, but Julian says that he
will never divulge them to the cold world.

The conclusion of the poem is clearly fictional. Not
only did Shelley revisit Venice several times after his
parting with Byron, but Byron's daughter Allegra
never succeeded in growing up. The first third of the
poem, then, is based on historical fact, modified
wherever it suits Shelley's convenience. The last third
is fiction. The question now is whether the lament
of the Maniac is fiction or fact.

---

tween Shelley and Allegra, but Shelley's letter does not mention any
such meeting. One difficulty is that a part of the pertinent letter is
missing. See *Letters,* IX, 328. Shelley may have derived his fictional
name from the Julian Alps, to which he alludes in this letter.

On this point Newman White has no doubts. In both versions of his life of Shelley he expresses his "practical certainty" that the Maniac's story has an autobiographical basis, that Shelley is describing there a "bitter . . . reality" in which he was the central figure.[9] It may be shown, on the contrary, that the story of the Maniac is not a picture of Shelley's secret thoughts about his own woes, but rather a semifictionalized treatment of the poet Tasso's imprisonment for real or alleged madness in the year 1579.

First, does the probable date of composition coincide with Shelley's interest in the life of Tasso? Shelley's own statement is that *Julian and Maddalo* was "written at Este," which establishes the date of composition between late August, when he accepted the loan of Byron's villa at Este, and early November, when he left Este for Naples. The description of the visit to Byron at Venice, hereinafter called the "conversation poem," was certainly composed after August 24, since it is based on the events which happened on August 23–24. The Maniac's lament may have been written in the August–November period, or it may have been substantially written at some earlier date in 1818, and then built into the conversation poem during the Este period. Either possibility fits the Tasso interpretation equally well, for it can be shown without difficulty that Shelley's interest in Tasso's life as the subject of a poem began in April, 1818, or perhaps earlier, and that his interest in Tasso continued until

9 Newman I. White, *Shelley* (2 vols., New York, 1940), II, 43. Cf. his *Portrait of Shelley* (New York, 1945), p. 286.

November, 1818, or perhaps later. The Este period, when Shelley said he wrote *Julian and Maddalo*, therefore falls within the period of Shelley's interest in Tasso, and the dates are right enough.

Second, how good is the evidence that Shelley was interested in Tasso's life as the subject of a poem? The inception of his interest in Tasso's biography, as opposed to Tasso's poetry, may very probably be dated from September 24, 1817, when he read Byron's *Lament of Tasso*, a complaint of 247 lines, mostly in heroic couplets. Here the imprisoned Tasso looks back over his unfortunate love affair with the Princess Leonora d'Este, sister of his patron, Alfonso of Ferrara, and consoles himself for his imprisonment by thinking on three satisfactions: he has completed his two great poems, *Aminta* and *Jerusalem Delivered;* he has forgiven Alfonso for placing him in a cell even though he must stay where he can hear the "long and maniac cry" of other "minds and bodies in captivity"; and he supposes that he will be buried near his beloved Leonora. Shelley was much impressed by this poem, but the section that particularly pleased him, as he told Byron, was that in which Tasso's "youthful feelings" were described. The lines which imply an "indistinct consciousness of its own greatness, which a heart of genius cherishes in solitude, amid neglect and contempt, have," said Shelley, "a profound and thrilling pathos which I will confess to you, whenever I turn to them, make my head wild with tears." [10] The lines

[10] *Letters,* IX, 245. Shelley knew Tasso as poet before he read Byron's *Lament.* Mary's reading lists show that he read *Jerusalem Delivered*

which so affected Shelley could only be 149–173, where Tasso is made to say that from birth his soul was "drunk with love," which mingled with all he saw and made him especially fond of natural objects and scenes. When his elders called him idler or punished him, he cursed them in his heart and retired to his bower to weep alone and dream again those "visions which arise without a sleep." He learned early the sorrows of spiritual isolation. Throughout his adolescence, his soul panted with indefinable longings, until at last he found what he had been seeking—the Princess Leonora, in whom he became so completely absorbed that he forgot nature and the world. Readers of Shelley's *Alastor* will not wonder that the poet should have been so much struck by this section of Byron's *Lament of Tasso*. Readers of the lament of the Maniac in *Julian and Maddalo* will perhaps recognize an allusion to Byron's poem in the Maniac's statement that "when a boy," he devoted his nature "to justice and to love," and that he was known as "that love-devoted youth." There are several obvious parallels of idea between Byron's *Lament of Tasso* and the lament of Shelley's Maniac. Both are imprisoned among other maniacs. Julian and Maddalo hear "fierce yells and howlings and lamentings keen," "moans, shrieks, and curses, and blaspheming prayers," as they ascend to the Maniac's apartment in the island madhouse. Byron's Tasso complains of "the long and maniac cry"

and *Aminta* in 1815, and that he returned to Tasso in 1816. On April 6, 1818, he began rereading *Aminta* with Mary, and at the same time took up a life of Tasso, probably that of Serassi, partly to practice his Italian.

of his fellow prisoners, and of the "lash and the increasing howl, And the half-inarticulate blasphemy." Byron's Tasso and Shelley's Maniac both begin by allusions to the unendurably slow passage of time, both long for the peace of the grave, and both close with the hope that death will come soon.

Soon after his arrival in Italy on March 30, 1818, and something over six months after his enthusiastic letter about Byron's poem, Shelley probably read Serassi's biography of Tasso, which he finished on April 11.[11] On April 20 he told Peacock that he meant to write a tragedy on Tasso's madness; on April 30 he told Hogg the same thing; and sometime in May he entered in a notebook, now at the Bodleian, brief notations for two scenes of the drama.[12] In one scene Tasso was to read a sonnet to Leonora; another scene was to deal with Tasso's famous visit to his sister Cornelia at Sorrento in July, 1577. Part of the week of May 11 Shelley spent in reading Count Manso's life of Tasso, and it was probably about this time that he composed the two fragments of the Tasso drama which have survived.[13] One of these is clearly the opening of the play. We are

[11] For Shelley's probable acquaintance with Serassi's *Vita* of Tasso, see C. B. Beall, *Modern Language Quarterly*, II (1941), 609–10. Twice in letters and twice in essays Shelley used a sentence attributed to Tasso which came from Serassi. Shelley might have found the sentence in Hobhouse, *Historical Illustrations of the Fourth Canto of Childe Harold* (2d ed., London, 1818), p. 26. Hobhouse is quoting from Serassi.

[12] *Letters,* IX, 298–99 and 307. The notebook entry is reprinted by A. Koszul, *Shelley's Prose in the Bodleian Manuscripts* (London, 1910), p. 148. The entry occurs at folio 41, ms. Shelley e.4.

[13] Mary's journal entry for May 4 records the reading of Manso's *Vita.*

introduced to several characters, one of whom is named Maddalo, and was probably intended to represent Count Maddalo Fucci, a historical character with whom Tasso once had a quarrel. The other fragment is a love song to Leonora. Shelley's interest in Tasso did not, however, cease at this point. In mid-July he spoke admiringly of Tasso's "delicate moral sensibility"; on August 16 he quoted a passage in Italian which he ascribed to Tasso, but which he had probably found in Serassi's life of Tasso.[14] When he visited Byron in Venice a week later he was disappointed that the *gondolieri,* who customarily entertained their passengers with recitations from Tasso, this time failed to do so.[15] In accepting Byron's villa at Este he entered a region filled with reminders of the Estensi, Tasso's patrons, and it was here by his own statement that he wrote *Julian and Maddalo.* On November 7, during the journey from Este to Naples, Shelley went sightseeing in Ferrara, inspected the mementoes of Tasso, visited Tasso's prison at the Hospital of Santa Anna, and sent Peacock "a piece of wood of the very door which for seven years and three months divided this glorious being from the air and the light." The Hospital was, thought Shelley, "a horrible abode for the . . . meanest thing that ever wore the shape of man, much more for one of delicate susceptibilities, and

14 *Letters,* IX, 312 and 321. Shelley repeated the phrase in altered form to Hunt, November, 1819. See *Letters,* X, 130. He also used it twice in his essays, once in the fragment "On Life" and again in the *Defence of Poetry.*
15 *Letters,* IX, 335 and note. Shelley's enthusiasm for Tasso as poet had given way by the fall of 1819 to admiration for Dante, Petrarch, and Boccaccio. See *Letters,* X, 86.

elevated fancies." [16] It is therefore evident that Shelley's interest in Tasso's life extended through a period of more than one year, that he seriously intended to write a drama on Tasso's madness, that he sketched out a curtain raiser and two later scenes, that he composed one love song to Leonora, that he read at least two biographies of Tasso, that he admired Tasso's delicate moral sensibility, and that even after the Este period, when *Julian and Maddalo* was written, he was sufficiently interested in Tasso so that in leaving Este for Naples he wished to stop at Ferrara to see the Tasso relics.

There is no way of knowing why Shelley abandoned his projected drama on Tasso. Both this play and that on the Biblical character Job were considered and laid aside in 1818, probably about the time that Shelley's interest in the *Prometheus Unbound* began to rise. But from what has been said it seems fairly clear that, as a substitute for the abandoned dramatic project, he embarked upon another, mainly modeled on Byron's *Lament of Tasso,* and partly based on the reading in Tasso's biography which he had done in preparation for the tragedy on Tasso's madness. The result was a lament only thirty lines shorter than Byron's poem, to which it bore some resemblance in its opening and closing passages; in the fact that it was presented, like most of Byron's poem, in heroic couplets; in the fact that it showed the protagonist imprisoned within earshot of the howls and blasphemies of other maniacal prisoners; and in the fact that it mentioned the pris-

[16] *Letters,* IX, 341.

oner's youthful devotion to love—a devotion, as we have seen, which Shelley found so moving in Byron's account that a reading of it made his head "wild with tears." Shelley's reason for concealing the Maniac's real identity can probably be found somewhere between his personal delight in mystifying even his closest friends, and a possible fear that he might be accused of imitating Byron's *Lament of Tasso*.

Two previous critics have implied or suggested that the Maniac was originally intended as a portrait of Tasso in a Ferrarese cell. Although Dowden was unwilling to guess at the identity of the Maniac, he suggested that some of Shelley's studies for the Tasso drama might have overflowed into the "mournful soliloquies" of *Julian and Maddalo*.[17] In 1930, R. D. Havens published an article in which he agreed with Dowden, pointed out that Shelley got the name Maddalo from his Tasso researches, and observed that while the Maniac's story contains no allusions to Tasso or Ferrara, nobody need be surprised, since in transferring the lines to his new piece, Shelley "would naturally drop or change all that were not adapted to it."[18] If either Dowden or Havens had taken note of the resemblance between Byron's *Lament of Tasso* and the Maniac's story, or if either of them had looked into Shelley's other source books, Manso's *Life of Tasso* and the work by Serassi, Professor White would in all conscience have been compelled to accept their conclusions, instead of merely admitting, as he does in a foot-

[17] Edward Dowden, *Life* (2 vols., 1886), II, 238.
[18] R. D. Havens, "Julian and Maddalo," *Studies in Philology*, XXVII (1930), 648–53.

note, the "possibility that Tasso was in Shelley's mind when he wrote, but in the background rather than in the foreground." [19]

It will be advisable to see, therefore, what data on Tasso Shelley could have assembled from a reading of the biographies by Manso and Serassi. According to the extremely cautious and circumspect life by Count Manso, Tasso pretended that he was in love with one of three ladies of the court of Ferrara, each of whom bore the name Leonora, in order to conceal which of the three was the real object of his passion. However, "alcuni credettero, che la dama di lui, sovra ogni altra amata, ed esaltata, fosse Madama Leonora d'Este, sorella del Duca Alfonso." [20] Manso adds his own opinion that Tasso's verses from Sorrento show that the Princess Leonora was "sua particolar Signora, e favoratrice"—that is, his own lady and favor-giver. But Tasso was a victim either of gossip or of organized conspiracy. One of his friends, "with whom he shared everything, even his thoughts, and from whom he had not completely concealed the secret of his loves . . . repeated one day some details of the amorous secrets of Tasso." Greatly angered, Tasso struck him in the face. In the duel which followed, Tasso was getting the best of it, when his opponents fled, escaping arrest by the Duke's men, who had been attracted to the spot by the clash of arms. Tasso was seized and placed in custody, not as a punishment for fighting but, as the diplomatic Manso points out, in order to protect him from

[19] White, *Shelley*, II, 558–59.
[20] Manso, *Vita*, in Tasso, *Opere* (Firenze, 1724), I, xvii.

potential assassins. Tasso failed to understand the motive behind his arrest, since the Duke appeared to be more incensed with him than a mere duel would warrant. Putting two and two together, he concluded that the Duke had heard of the gossip which had caused the fight: that is, the statement that he was in love with a lady of the ducal court.[21] We are left to infer that the Ferrarese "gentleman" babbled about Tasso's secret love for the Princess Leonora, and that the arrest and imprisonment were, in Tasso's mind, a penalty for having allowed this affair to reach the public ear. Tasso soon broke prison and fled Ferrara. But he chose for his return the inauspicious moment of the Duke's third marriage. The former favorite of the court was received with such coldness that he gave vent to his indignation and was again imprisoned, this time for seven years in the Hospital of Santa Anna. Manso attributes this second imprisonment to the Duke's magnanimous desire to restore Tasso's disturbed imagination to normal. Yet the biographer contrives to be so ambiguous in what he says of Tasso's madness that he seems to be attempting to leave room for the widely accepted story (noted by Quadrio and Baruffaldi) that Tasso was only feigning insanity upon instructions from the Duke. According to the agreement, so long as Tasso pretended to be out of his mind the Duke would keep him in pleasant apartments in the prison, but would not invoke the death penalty, which would otherwise be the inevitable consequence of Tasso's having cast a blot on the scutcheon of the proud House

21 *Ibid.*, xxiv–vi.

of Este. But while Manso appears to be of two minds on the insanity question, he has much to say about the apparitions or phantasms which appeared to Tasso, among whom the Devil was a prominent visitor.

Serassi, who was very probably the third main source of Shelley's knowledge of Tasso, agrees with Manso at many points, but rejects the implication that there was any real love affair between Tasso and the Princess. At the same time, he refuses to believe that Tasso was insane, for he thinks such poetry as Tasso's could hardly have been composed by a diseased mind. Even the level-headed Serassi finds it hard to avoid being touched by the romantic story. He notes the constancy of Tasso's devotion to Leonora, and describes the Princess as very beautiful, graceful, modest, and reserved, and given to improving her mind by learned converse with literary men.[22]

All of the necessary hints for the lament of Shelley's Maniac can be found either in Byron's *Lament of Tasso,* or in the lives of Tasso by Serassi and Count Manso. The Maniac begins, as in Byron, with a remark about the slow passage of time in prison. He mentions the "mask of falsehood" which he must wear, concealing the truth even from his friends. This is a clear allusion to the tradition that Tasso's madness was feigned, a view implied in Manso and Serassi, and stated outright three times in Byron's *Lament of Tasso.*[23] The Maniac says that if he made an error, he has had nothing out of it but pain, insult, unrest, and

[22] Serassi, *Vita* (1790), pp. 149–50.
[23] *Lament of Tasso,* lines 4, 48, 214.

terror. He has not bought repentance with pleasure or "a dark yet sweet offense." He invokes his "spirit's mate" as one who would weep if she knew the true extent of "her lost friend's incommunicable woe." But he will not yield to scorn or hate, which are poor medicines for a mind which scorn and hate have wounded. Here Shelley is closely following Byron. Byron's lamenter admits that he was delirious to aspire to so lofty a love as Leonora, for his life has been blighted, his reputation debased, and his thoughts branded as things to shun and fear. Yet he feels no remorse, having no cause.[24] If it was presumptuous in him to love without design, that sad fatality has cost him dear.[25] But he holds no grudges: he has cast all bitterness from his heart, and even though Leonora will not pity him, he cannot forsake her memory. Despite his sufferings, Shelley's Maniac has not changed his basic beliefs or resolutions; he will not sanction tyranny or surrender to avarice, misanthropy, or lust. He longs for the peace of the grave. Byron's Tasso is still too proud to be vindictive; he has pardoned the insults of the Prince, and longs only for death.

In the midst of the Maniac's soliloquy, his fancy becomes overwrought, and he thinks he sees beside him the phantasm of his beloved. She has taken Death for her paramour, and the Maniac says that he will watch from his winding sheet as she makes the tomb her bridal bed. Manso, as we have seen, describes Tasso's hallucinations at some length. Byron's Tasso com-

24 *Ibid.,* lines 47–100.
25 *Ibid.,* lines 140–41.

plains that his mind plays him tricks. Unwonted lights
shine along his prison and a "strange demon" vexes
him. Shelley may also have remembered, with some
horror, the closing lines of Byron's poem, where Tasso
imagines that he and Leonora will be entwined forever—in the grave. When the phantasm disappears,
Shelley's Maniac says that it has acted like a serpent,
poisoning the very breast that warmed it. He recalls
the lady's former protest that he did not love her
enough; yet he loved her even to his overthrow, while
she would like now to forget her former protestation.
If they had never met and embraced, he would not
have been plagued with present agonies, nor would
she have had to endure his love while her own for him
was diminishing, nor could she taunt him for imagin-
ing that one of his personal appearance should address
himself to "love's work." Here Shelley is outreaching
Byron. The Maniac's lady evidently encouraged his
love, but grew cold after the love was consummated.
Byron's Leonora was never an active participant, but
only a shrine to be worshiped from a distance. Yet
Byron's Tasso accuses Leonora of undue pride of sta-
tion, and of being ashamed that such a one as he could
love her.[26] The Maniac's statement that he was not
personally attractive could have been derived from
Manso's very detailed description of Tasso, where the
poet is said to have been tall and well proportioned,
but where such other details as his large nose and
mouth, thick prominent teeth and thin lips, the depression in his forehead, the peculiar slope of his

[26] *Lament of Tasso,* lines 228–30.

head, and his sparse black eyebrows, do not add up, whatever the Count's intention, to a vision of male beauty.[27]

In the remaining lines spoken by Shelley's Maniac, other Byronic echoes occur. As the Maniac writes, his eyes are dazzled with tears. Byron's Tasso blots with tears the final page of his masterwork. Shelley's Maniac says that he has refrained from suicide in order that his lady will be less desolate. Byron's Tasso will not "sanction with self-slaughter" the lying statement that he is insane. Shelley's Maniac says that he has hidden every spark of the love which consumes him under the embers of his words. Byron's Tasso says that he has breathed no word of a love which was "sufficient to itself, its own reward." Shelley's Maniac concludes by calling for death. Byron's Tasso concludes with thoughts of the grave where he and Leonora will be buried under the same laurel tree.

In short, it would appear that the key poem in solving the mystery of the identity of Shelley's Maniac is Byron's *Lament of Tasso,* though Shelley's knowledge of Serassi and Manso was doubtless useful to him in completing his conception of the character. From the foregoing argument that the Maniac's lament in *Julian and Maddalo* is Shelley's own version of *The Lament of Tasso,* framed with a story which is partly autobiographical and partly fictional, the present investigation can now be directed to Professor White's argument that it is a "practical certainty that the Madman's

[27] *Julian and Maddalo,* lines 463–66. Cf. Manso, *Vita,* in Tasso, *Opere,* I, lxxv.

story is autobiographical," and that it stems from the
spiritual dichotomy which seems to have occurred between Shelley and his wife Mary at a date which, according to White, was not very far removed from that
on which the *Julian and Maddalo* was composed.

Nobody can blame a biographer for making out the
best possible argument for a position he has adopted
after due contemplation of the available facts. But the
whole case for the connection between the Maniac's
complaint and the alleged spiritual divorce of Shelley
and Mary rests on very flimsy evidence. The facts appear to prove rather that the abysmal spiritual despondency in Mary, to which her husband often alludes
while it is present, did not really take effect until the
following summer, between June and August, 1819,
after the death of her second child, William.[28] If, there-

[28] There is no dependable evidence of a protracted or abnormal depression of spirits in either Shelley or Mary during the fall of 1818.
Mary's despondency, which no doubt resulted in somewhat strained
personal relations with her husband, clearly occurred in the five-
month period between June 7, 1819, when her second child, William,
died, and November 12, when her third child, Percy, was born.
Shelley states (Julian *Letters* IX, 333) that the death of Clara on September 24, 1818, "reduced Mary to a kind of despair," but she evidently made a fair recovery from this first blow. On April 6, 1819,
she says that she suffers from "ill spirits," though "God knows why,"
and evil thoughts hang about her "only now and then" (*Letters of
Mary W. Shelley,* ed. F. L. Jones, I, 66–67). On April 26, she says
that she is in "better health and spirits." But William's death in June
produced terrible suffering. "I feel it more now than at Rome," she
wrote on June 27; "the thought never leaves me for a single moment"
(Jones, *op. cit.,* I, 73–74). Other letters both by Shelley (Julian *Letters,* X, 53, 58, 60, 64, 66–68, 87) and by Mary (Jones, *op. cit.,* I, 75, 79,
81) allude to the awful depression of spirits in Mary during these
months. Professor Elizabeth Nitchie's valuable article, *Studies in
Philology,* XL (1943), 447–462, indicates that Mary sought to work
out her despair by writing the semiautobiographical story "Mathilda"

fore, as Shelley himself says, *Julian and Maddalo* was composed at Este in September or October, 1818, it could have had nothing to do with the spiritual dissociation of which White makes so much.

White believes that the death of little Clara Shelley on September 24, 1818, was the real inception of the Shelleys' marital difficulties, or at least of Shelley's period of great mental dejection. "On the surface," says White, "both Shelley and Mary were stoically silent. But beneath the surface was a deep feeling of misery that was to have a far more important effect upon the events of the next few months than the trivial details that Mary so mechanically set down in her journal or the sightseeing that Shelley recorded so calmly in his letters to Peacock." [29] Except for the questionable statement that the bereaved parents were stoically silent, this is guesswork. How does White or any man know what was beneath the surface of the parents' minds? They both kept busy reading and writing; they visited their friends in Venice; they wrote their friends in England; they went sightseeing; Mary made entries in her journal. But nowhere is there tangible evidence of a feeling of misery deep enough to cause a split between husband and wife.

---

between August 4 and September 12, 1819. Although Mary's pregnancy doubtless contributed to her "ill spirits," the birth of her second son saw an almost immediate improvement in her state of mind.

[29] White, *Shelley*, II, 40. Two weeks after Clara's death, as was perfectly natural, Shelley remarked to Peacock (Oct. 8, 1818) that they had "all had bad spirits enough" and that he had also been in bad health. But he added that he *intended* to be better soon. The statement hardly indicates abnormal despondency, but rather a determination to throw off his afflictions.

The next step in White's argument is also open to question. "There is no indication in Mary's journal or elsewhere that dates *Julian and Maddalo* definitely before or after September 24." This is true. But White continues, "Beginning with *Julian and Maddalo* and *Lines Written among the Euganean Hills,* and for some months thereafter, his personal poems reached their greatest depths of despondency. If we include *Julian and Maddalo,* Shelley completed seven poems in 1818 after Clara Shelley's death, and every single one of them is tinged with the same melancholy and despondence." To this it should be objected that the admittedly autobiographical portion of *Julian and Maddalo* is rather optimistic than otherwise, and that Julian, who represents Shelley, despite his fundamentally serious character, is not at all depressed during his visit to Maddalo. Furthermore, no good reason to call the story of the Maniac "personal" has yet been advanced. Furthermore, although White asserts rightly that there is no way of dating *Julian and Maddalo* in its entirety either before or after Clara's death, one should notice his tacit assumption at the end of the same paragraph that *Julian and Maddalo* belongs after Clara's death. One has in mind the statement that "If we include *Julian and Maddalo,* Shelley completed seven poems in 1818 after Clara Shelley's death." His further statement that "every one of [these poems] is tinged with the same melancholy and despondence" is open to the objection that it may not be the "same" melancholy at all, but a melancholy of quite different origin in each of the poems.

White's third step appears to leave the way open for some other interpretation than an autobiographical one. At the same time, by inserting the phrase about the Maniac's "extreme dejection," he continues to make upon the reader the impression that the autobiographical interpretation is the correct one. "If *Julian and Maddalo* was written before the death of Clara," says White, "the extreme dejection expressed throughout most of its length by the Madman is either non-autobiographical or else must be referred to some other cause than the death of Clara." [30] To this it must be objected that extreme dejection is not expressed by the Madman throughout most of the length of the poem. For the poem is 618 lines long, and the Madman's speech occupies only 209 of these lines, or roughly a third of the poem, which is certainly not most of the length of *Julian and Maddalo*. Furthermore there is no mark of "extreme dejection" elsewhere in the poem, so that the third step in White's argument is simply untrue. But White closes this paragraph with another reference to the "important hidden forces which both Shelley and Mary rigorously excluded from their letters and journal," hidden forces for which, as we have shown, there is no evidence beyond the biographer's guesswork.

The fourth step in White's argument is an attempt to account for the discrepancy in tone between the Julian and Maddalo story and the Maniac's lament. "It is quite possible," says White, "(and, I suspect, likely) that Shelley set out to write a poem about his conversa-

[30] White, *Shelley*, II, 42.

tions with Byron, that the first third of the poem was
written in this serene, unclouded spirit—and that
something then occurred which completely changed
the tone and made it in the end a very different poem
from the one originally intended. In this case the first
third of the poem must have been written before
Clara's death, and the remainder, totally changed by
that event and its consequences, soon afterwards." It is
of course obvious that Shelley set out to write a poem
about his conversations with Byron, and that he completed the first third of it in a serene unclouded spirit.
But in implying that the change in tone was oc-
casioned by Clara's death, and that the first and last
parts of the poem were therefore written before and
after her death, respectively, White is again, and one is
sorry to repeat the statement, only guessing.

But by this time White has evidently convinced himself that the Madman's story is autobiographical. For
he goes on to say that his supposition as to the dates
of the two parts into which he separates the poem "is
supported by the practical certainty that the Madman's story is autobiographical." [31] He gives four
reasons for believing that this is a "practical certainty,"
and it will be well to examine them in order to see
whether they clinch his argument. The first reason is
this: "The intense dejection of the Madman, cor-
responding as it does with the professedly personal
passages of the same sort that dominated Shelley's
poetry for the next few months, strongly suggests an
autobiographical basis." To this reason it may be

[31] White, *Shelley*, II, 43.

answered that White has not educed any evidence to
show that Shelley was deeply dejected during the Este
period, though one must admit that the *Lines Written
among the Euganean Hills,* dated October, 1818, although basically "optimistic," is not a serene and unclouded poem, and the letter to Peacock shows that
Shelley felt anything but gay over his baby's death. Yet
even with this admission, White has admittedly no
evidence to prove that the composition of the Madman's story belongs to the period after September 24,
or even that it was written at Este, for Shelley's statement that *Julian and Maddalo* was written at Este
might mean only that the Maniac's story and the poem
on the conversations with Byron were *put together* at
Este. It is not out of the question, in view of the dates
of Shelley's interest in Tasso, that a preliminary draft
of the Maniac's story had been made prior to the Este
period.

The second reason for a biographical interpretation
of the Madman's story is this: "In his letters Shelley
once referred to the poem as being based on actual
fact, and once to the Madman as a real person, like
Julian and Maddalo." To this statement it may be
rejoined that Tasso, was, in his time, as real a person
as Julian and Maddalo, and that in Shelley's mind, at
any rate, the data on the life of Tasso which he had
gleaned from Byron, Manso, and Serassi, were "actual
fact."

White's third and fourth reasons are both concerned
with the resemblance between some statements which
are made about the Madman and some statements

which Shelley makes about himself in other "professedly autobiographical" poems. Reason three is that
"In the poem Maddalo first speaks of the Madman as
having been once very like Julian (Shelley), and the
Madman himself refers to his youthful self-dedication
to love and justice, as Shelley had twice before in professedly autobiographical passages commemorated his
own youthful self-dedication." Reason four is that the
Madman's "general character is strikingly similar to
the traits that Shelley later assigned to himself in
Adonais and 'Ode to the West Wind.' " To both these
arguments it may be answered that one of the reasons
for Shelley's attraction to Tasso as a historical character was that he discerned in the elder poet some resemblances to his own cast of mind. When he read
Byron's *Lament of Tasso* he was especially impressed
by those portions of the poem in which Tasso's youthful self-dedication to love (though not to justice) is
touchingly set forth. These lines made Shelley's head
"wild with tears." Why? One might suppose that he
reacted in this fashion for the very good reason that he
saw in Tasso's youth, as Byron described it, a kind of
similarity to his own. Thus the first of White's four
reasons rests on guesswork as to the date of composition of the Madman's story, and the other three reasons
are just as good reasons for believing that the Madman
was Tasso as that the Madman was Shelley.

White's conclusion is that "the centre of the poem
. . . is an autobiographical portrait of Shelley in the
grip of a 'dreadful . . . reality.' What this 'reality'
was for the Madman may not be literally the same as

what it was for his prototype, Shelley; but whatever it was, it was the dominant fact in Shelley's life for several very important months and lies at the root of his most despondent personal poetry." White then expends eight more pages upon a speculative interpretation of the poem's text, through which one need not follow him—first because, as he himself admits with characteristic honesty, it is "an excursion into subjective interpretation" which he "fully realizes may be highly treacherous"; and second because it has been, one hopes, sufficiently shown that White is on very treacherous footing indeed, and that his whole body of "evidence" for a "spiritual divorce" involves a transfer back to the Este period of a deep dejection of spirits in Mary which did not demonstrably come until several months later, although White would like to believe, for the purposes of his own interpretation, that it began in Mary's alleged coldness immediately after Clara's death. White concludes that Shelley is addressing the "Mary-that-was" as his true spiritual mate, while the figure we have called the phantasm represents Mary at a later date, "turned temporarily into a strange antagonistic personality by her grief." But there is far better reason to believe that the Maniac's lady is the "Leonora-that-was," being recalled by Tasso from his prison.

In singling out Professor White as the object of attention, and in not giving serious consideration to the autobiographical interpretations offered by Salt, Peck, Grabo, and John Harrington Smith, the purpose has has been to concentrate on the author of the best and

most influential biography of Shelley.[32] These commentators agree that the Maniac is Shelley, and disa-
gree only, or chiefly, in variously identifying the
Maniac's lady as Harriet Westbrook, or as Mary Shelley, or as Claire Clairmont. One would hope that the
case for Tasso as the original of the Maniac is now so
plain that no further guesswork as to the identity of
the mysterious lady is required. She is the Princess
Leonora d'Este, as Shelley imagined her after reading
Byron's *Lament of Tasso,* and the lives of Tasso by
Serassi and Count Manso.

The foregoing discussion has, of course, an important bearing on the question as to how far, for critical purposes, the allegedly autobiographical passages
in Shelley's poems may be trusted. It proves that such
passages are not at all trustworthy in determining the
actual circumstances and the actual state of mind in
which Shelley composed a given poem. The discussion
has an even more important bearing on the related
question as to how far, for biographical purposes, allegedly autobiographical passages in the poetry can be

[32] Among reputable scholars there have been three main schools of
thought as to the identity of the Maniac's lady. H. S. Salt, *Percy
Bysshe Shelley: A Monograph* (London, 1888), pp. 246–49, concludes
that the episode is "an idealized description of Shelley's disastrous
marriage with Harriet Westbrook." W. E. Peck, *Shelley: His Life
and Work,* II, 104–5, follows Salt. Carl Grabo, *The Magic Plant*
(Chapel Hill, N.C., 1936), pp. 267–71, states that "the personal facts
underlying the story may have had something to do with Shelley's
belief that Mary no longer loved him," but adds that "Shelley may
be writing of someone unknown and unguessed." White takes up
where Grabo leaves off. More recently, J. H. Smith, "Shelley and
Claire Clairmont," *PMLA,* LIV (1939), 785–815, has suggested that
the Maniac's lady is probably Claire.

safely utilized in reading one's way beneath the surface of a life. Even when a biographer proceeds, as has Professor White, with the utmost caution, buttressing his position with qualifications, the dangers are many and the possibility always remains that another ghost than that of autobiography will rise to walk the castle ramparts.[33]

[33] Much of what R. M. Smith and his associates have to say about White's *Shelley* is unfair, but a part of their statement about *Julian and Maddalo* appears to be supported by the facts here discovered: "With the artist we can never be sure where reality ends and imagination begins. Particularly is this true of Shelley, who was not only a mythmaker but the cause of mythmaking in others. . . . It is disconcerting, therefore, to find White subjecting *Julian and Maddalo* to such treatment in a tortuous effort to sustain his notions about Mary, Clara, and Elena Adelaide in the Hoppner affair" (Smith, *et al., The Shelley Legend*, p. 305).

William Butler Yeats

꧁

By MARION WITT

NOT ALL POETS—in fact, not many poets—have been engaged to the degree that Yeats was in dramatizing their own lives. In 1914 Yeats wrote in *Reveries over Childhood and Youth* of his early discovery that personal utterance, what his father called "only egotism," could be "as fine an escape from rhetoric or abstraction as drama itself." [1] From the point when he made this discovery, Yeats said, he tried to write out of his emotions exactly as they came to him in life. To himself he repeated his credo: "If I can be sincere and make my language natural, and without becoming discursive, like a novelist, and so indiscreet and prosaic, I shall, if good luck or bad luck make my life interesting, be a great poet; for it will be no longer a matter of literature at all." During most of his career Yeats maintained this very close relationship between his life and his poetry.

[1] Passages in this paper from W. B. Yeats, *Autobiography; Essays; A Vision; Collected Poems; The King of the Great Clock Tower, Commentaries and Poems;* and *Last Poems and Plays* are quoted with the kind permission of The Macmillan Company, publishers.

Yeats himself believed that the facts about his life and thought would be important to his readers. In the preface to *The Trembling of the Veil* (1922) he said that "the life of a man of genius, because of his greater sincerity, is often an experiment that needs analysis and record." He referred to his friends but in practice applied the notion to himself. His long autobiography, his many prefaces and the annotations of his poetry, his diaries, his essays, his letters, *A Vision*—all these are filled with the account of his outer and inner life.

Yet, in spite of this rich autobiographical material, now, nearly eight years after Yeats's death, the complete story of his life has not been told. Among materials yet unpublished and still largely inaccessible are several important items. A very large collection of diaries, letters, manuscripts in prose and verse is now in Mrs. Yeats's possession. In an article published early this year, Mr. A. Norman Jeffares gives tantalizing samples of the manuscripts Mrs. Yeats has and reports that she saved even torn fragments, reduced them to order, and has established many dates. Mr. Joseph Hone, the official biographer, had access to these manuscripts, but Hone's life of Yeats, informative as it is, is characterized by tactful omissions. Though a considerable group of Yeats's letters have been printed, a full collection has not. The so-called Dublin edition of all Yeats's work, which Scribner's will publish in this country, is to be equipped with new prefaces Yeats wrote in the last years of his life and also the final corrected text of his poetry. Of these prefaces Yeats told Lady Gerald Wellesley when he was working on them in 1937 that one might "develop into an essay on the nature of poetry." The letters, the definitive edition with its prefaces, the manuscripts Mrs. Yeats has— all these, when and if they are printed, may change in some degree our conception of Yeats the man and poet. If I may hazard a guess, the change will not be radical. Certainly, however, the new material will enrich our knowledge of the man, increase our understanding of the poetry.

Of experiences in Yeats's life which overflow in his poetry several are especially interesting to that hypothetical reader who approaches the *Collected Poems* or *Collected Plays* with no knowledge at all of the poet. First among these would be his relation to the Ireland in which he grew up, which he by turns loved and hated, idealized and reviled, but never to the end abandoned as a theme. Ireland is closely connected with the beautiful and fiery patriot, Maud Gonne, and only an entirely incurious reader could fail to wish to know more than Yeats tells in his verse of that trouble of his life. In Ireland, too, Yeats found or evolved his concept of aristocracy and nobility, his romantic exaltation of the peasantry, his hatred of the mob, the dull, leveling middle classes. All these themes appear constantly in his poetry, and knowledge of their sources in Yeats's life reveals the integrity of the poems. The friends who people Yeats's pages are perhaps idealized, certainly simplified, and notes on them as they were provide illumination. Most significant of all in understanding many difficult poems is Yeats's search for a philosophy and a religion, his constant preoccupation with the supernatural from his boyhood to the grave.

First, the poems about Ireland reveal a constant antithesis in Yeats's thought and feeling about his native land. He repeatedly insisted that all his work was done for Ireland and that he would write in love or in hate for his own people. This nationalism was based in his divided childhood, with winters in gray London among the English he scorned and summers in the Sligo he longed for. The child, who felt, as his aunt warned him he would, a nobody in London, saw Sligo and Ireland in a romantic haze. When in old age Yeats knew that the justice and honesty and passion he wanted have no connection with race or country, when he wrote to Lady Gerald Wellesley that though he made the "necessary senatorial speech" in Dublin, he was "anarchic as a sparrow," he nevertheless clung to his old Irish nationalism, to his old concept of race:

> Many times man lives and dies
> Between his two eternities,
> That of race and that of soul,
> And ancient Ireland knew it all.
> —*Under Ben Bulben*

In the early nineties Yeats wrote sentimental verses about modern Ireland and its "dear old places," its "men who love the cause that never dies." These verses exist only in the early volumes, for those reprinted in *Collected Poems* are radically altered in tone and substance. He dreamed as a young man that Ireland might have a unity of culture because, he said, she had turned so willingly from the "bragging rhetoric and

gregarious humour of O'Connell's generation and
school" to the "solitary and proud Parnell as to her
anti-self." But this dream passed quickly. Parnell was
repudiated and died. All in Ireland, according to
Yeats, gave way to abstraction and hatred, to violence
on the one hand, to continued vulgarization of art on
the other: to plots to blow up ancient houses (these
plots made, by the way, by charming old men who believed in fairies) or to pepper pots made in the form of
a round tower with a wolf-dog at its foot. And this un-
reconciled struggle, intensified in Yeats's mind by the
fact that it absorbed the most beautiful woman of her
time and the love of his life, was the center of his own
existence for twenty years from 1889 to the death of
Synge in 1909. During all Yeats's long work for Ireland,
in founding Irish literary societies in London and Dublin, in work for the Wolfe Tone Memorial Committee
in 1898, in his arduous work for the Irish theatre, he
was always of divided mind. His friends, especially
Maud Gonne, urged political action first, with literature as a handmaid to politics; but he firmly believed
that bad art could never serve Ireland's cause. Many
poems came from a basic division in Yeats's feeling
about Ireland: that Ireland was indeed a heroine
named Cathleen ni Houlihan tormented by the black
villain, England; and, conversely, that too many of the
Irish fought fanatically and without honor.

The great reflowering of Yeats's poetry dates from
his renunciation of an active part in the Irish struggle,
from the beginning of his record in poetry of the
emotions that fight roused in him. In many poems,

from 1909 to 1920—and indeed thereafter—Yeats attacked the rancorous, leveling mob, the half-educated middle classes who slip easily, he said, into "pedantry, which opens to the mind a kind of sensual ease." Before one finds this repudiation of the people mere snobbery, it is important to remember the bitterness of some of Yeats's experiences with them. He learned first in England of the power of the popular press and of popular and pedantic writers like Mrs. Humphry Ward in Aubrey Beardsley's tragic life and death. During the fight over his own *Countess Cathleen* in Dublin, a cardinal denounced a play he had neither read nor seen; and journalists, in libelous pamphlets, attributed to Yeats opinions he had put dramatically in the mouths of demons. Rancor ran even wilder in the controversy over the *Playboy,* both in Ireland and in America. A little later when Sir Hugh Lane, Lady Gregory's nephew, desired to make a munificent gift of modern French paintings to Ireland, he was accused of trying to enrich himself at Ireland's expense. Nobody, said his enemies, gives away seventy thousand pounds. Lane was insulted, even harried out of Ireland. As early as 1905 Yeats wrote to John Quinn, "We will have a hard fight before we get the right of every man to see the world in his own way admitted." That fight was never won in Ireland. As senator of the Irish Free State, Yeats found the ministers in De Valera's government shared his attitude toward censorship but dared not act for fear of the people. The mob still reigned, and in 1934 Yeats wrote that unless that reign were broken, Irish men of letters would "live like outlaws in their own country." As late as 1937 he told Dorothy Wellesley of his great dejection, a major reason being the slanderous and threatening attacks on him and his friends in the Dublin press. Poems scorning the middle classes who beat down great art, who have a "self-complacent certainty that all had been arranged, all provided for, all set out in clear type in manual of devotion or in doctrine," who share a passion for leveling, who fumble in a greasy till and burn holy candles, who accuse all differers of base intent, who have no honor and are in no way disgraced if proved to be without honor—all these opinions and feelings are based on Yeats's or his friends' experiences. It must be said, too, that he wrote more often in defense of his friends than of himself. As an old man he advised poets to

> Wander in dreams no more;
> What if the Church and the State
> Are the mob that howls at the door!
> —*"Here is fresh matter, poet"*

In direct antithesis to the hated mob are Yeats's symbols of Irish greatness: Parnell because he was passionate, proud, and solitary and yet worked for the Irish cause; John O'Leary, the old Fenian, because his detachment from his own patriotic enthusiasms gave his mind, according to Yeats, a curious and solitary distinction. Parnell was a natural choice as symbol of the noble Irishman howled down by the mob, as in the distinguished poem, *To a Shade,* the occasion of which was Hugh Lane's miserable experience. Yeats's reasons for choosing O'Leary for a similar role are not evident in the poems but made clear in the *Autobiography* and elsewhere. Yeats actually lived in O'Leary's Dublin house in the nineties, acknowledged his leadership gladly, and said later that all he had set his hand to had come from O'Leary's teaching. He described O'Leary as the handsomest old man he ever saw, a man of stoic fortitude under imprisonment, a man of highest moral code and courage. Yeats wrote in 1897: "Our public men, with the exception of Mr. John O'Leary, have been afraid to differ from the people in anything, and now we haven't got a pensworth of respect for anybody but Mr. John O'Leary." He alone, Yeats added, can tell the Irish the difference between right and wrong. O'Leary said, "There are things a man may not do to save his country," and he warned an Irishman who fought for the Pope against the Italian peasants that trying to oppress others was a poor preparation for freeing his own land. O'Leary objected to bombing and dynamiting, carefully defined the limits of what he called honorable warfare, and was never afraid to assert his strong views. Yeats found in O'Leary his ideal for Ireland and for himself: a detachment from his own enthusiasms to breed a curious and solitary distinction, a sense of values beyond fanatic nationalism. In the poem *September, 1913,* Yeats wrote,

> Romantic Ireland's dead and gone,
> It's with O'Leary in the grave,

and in *Last Poems* "O'Leary's noble head" is the first of "Beautiful, Lofty Things."

The characteristic antithesis of Yeats's thought and

feeling about Irish nationalism pervades the poems inspired by the Easter Rebellion of 1916, and only his experiences of the preceding quarter-century make clear the reason for the antithesis. Of the sixteen leaders of the rebellion who were executed, Yeats names in the poem *Easter, 1916* four he knew personally: Thomas MacDonagh, James Connolly, Patrick Pearse, John MacBride. Of them all Yeats wrote elsewhere, and Pearse is vividly pictured in Sean O'Casey's recent book, *Drums under the Window,* as a dreamer pulled separate ways by two attractions: St. Patrick's robe and "the spear of danger held out to him by the singing, laughing, battling boy Cuchullain." Pearse and MacDonagh were gentle men, but both of them had hearts hardened to a stone by one purpose. So, too, had Connolly, the practical labor leader, and MacBride, the "drunken, vainglorious lout," who married Maud Gonne and made her wretched. In connection with *Easter, 1916,* Yeats tells in the *Autobiography,* also, of an old Irish Member of Parliament who before the Irish Literary Society in London recited a ballad in the oratorical, sentimental manner of Young Ireland, repeated his sacred names of Wolfe Tone, Emmet, Owen Roe, and mourned that the new poets like Yeats had taken some of that sacredness away. Yeats said his conscience troubled him for years and that he had that old politician in mind when he wrote in *Easter, 1916:*

> . . . Our part
> To murmur name upon name,
> As a mother names her child

When sleep at last has come
On limbs that had run wild. . . .

I write it out in a verse—
MacDonagh and MacBride
And Connolly and Pearse
Now and in time to be,
Wherever green is worn,
Are changed, changed utterly:
A terrible beauty is born.

To the end, Yeats was to love, to admire, to envy the
man of action against the man of thought; yet the man
of action was too often driven, as he saw it, by fanatic
opinion that makes a stone of the heart. His envy of the
man of action appears in *Meditations in Time of Civil
War;* and in *Last Poems* Connolly and Pearse are
praised unreservedly as men of action. But in 1916 the
critical side of Yeats's mind had to ask, "Was it need-
less death after all?" Mr. L. A. G. Strong tells how a
few years later someone asked Yeats at Oxford, "Are
you not afraid, Sir, that your thought will lead you
away from the realities of life, into some intellectual
desert, remote from action?" The poet's reply was,
"No. Too many of my friends have been shot." Conversely, Mrs. Yeats says that when her husband was
correcting the proofs of *Collected Poems* in 1933 he
remarked, "I have spent my life saying the same things
in different ways. I denounced old age before I was
twenty, and the swordsman throughout repudiates the
saint—though with vacillation." This very vacillation
is the theme of *Easter, 1916.*

Nothing in Yeats's life so permeated his lyrics as his

long, unsatisfied love for Maud Gonne. A great many
poems, from the volume of 1892 to *Last Poems* in
1940, are devoted to her. In addition, her sacrificial
charities to peasants in Donegal produced *The Countess Cathleen,* a vision of impossibly beautiful life with
her *The Land of Heart's Desire.* Her patriotic enthusiasm motivated *Cathleen ni Houlihan,* in which
she played the title role, and Mr. Louis MacNeice
thinks Forgael's search for ideal love in *The Shadowy
Waters* is a further echo of Yeats's devotion. What was
she really, this woman who inspired the finest love
poetry of this century?

Of her beauty Yeats recorded much. Her apple-
blossom skin, her golden-brown hair, her great stature,
her grace of movement were real enough. Bernard
Shaw said she was "outrageously beautiful." The
photograph she used as a frontispiece to her autobiography, *A Servant of the Queen* (1938), is of a
young, conventionally beautiful woman with a smugly
untouched and thoughtless face. It is, in fact, the face
of a woman who in old age would write of herself that
when she learned nationalism at the feet of John
O'Leary, she was so beautiful that nobody noticed her
Paris clothes. Her autobiography and the sketch she
contributed to *Scattering Branches,* supposedly on
Yeats but largely on herself, give little hint of the
charm and distinction Yeats found in her; but both
of these were written when she was an old woman.

Her power of oratory swayed vast crowds in Ireland
and France. Her grace, her beauty, her sweet, low voice

suggested to the crowd, Yeats said, something they had created and loved. He recorded one of her speeches in a report on her sent in 1892 to the Boston *Pilot*. It shows that willingness to lie for a cause which made Synge loathe her. That she loved excitement, even notoriety, is witnessed by many who knew her in the years Yeats followed her train. George Pollexfen, Yeats's uncle, heard a story of how Maud Gonne applauded when some one called out "Shoot him!" directed at an Irish landlord. Pollexfen's dry comment was, "It's wonderful what some people will do for notoriety."

The aspect of her character Yeats stresses most is her fanaticism: "Women," he said, "give all to opinion as to some terrible stone doll." She praised war not as a creator of virtue but as if there were some virtue in the excitement of war itself. She exulted in glass-breaking at Victoria's Jubilee in Dublin, she conspired to sink British troop ships in the Boer War, she worked for years to secure a French invasion of Ireland. She proposed to send eighty pugilists in place of the Irish members to the House of Commons. These pugilists were to be paid by results. According to her enemies, she taught thousands of Irish children to answer a catechism which began, "What is the origin of evil?" "England." She said herself, "Every one must work according to his temperament. . . . I never willingly discouraged a Dynamiter or a constitutionalist, a realist or a lyrical writer. My chief preoccupation was how their work could help forward the Irish separatist movement." Her chief encouragement was to violent action. It was no poetic fantasy that she "taught to ignorant men most violent ways." Yeats spoke truth, too, when he wrote:

> My darling cannot understand
> What I have done, or what would do
> In this blind bitter land.
>
> —*Words*

It is not surprising that O'Leary, that stern moralist, repudiated her ("She is no disciple of mine," he said), and mourned over Yeats's devotion to her.

There is an element of humorous truth in what Maud Gonne said to Yeats: "You make poetry out of what you call your unhappiness and you are happy in that." Yet only a hard woman could have spoken these words to a man really suffering from hopeless love, and, worse still, have recorded them with pride a generation later. She records, too, that when she was recovering from a serious illness in France, Yeats's great concern, expressed in *A Dream of Death,* she found "very amusing." Remarks like these underline such a stanza as

> Like the moon her kindness is,
> If kindness I may call
> What has no comprehension in't,
> But is the same for all
> As though my sorrow were a scene
> Upon a painted wall.
>
> —*A Man Young and Old*

Maud Gonne's condescension to "Willie Yeats" in all she has written of him is more than a little trying, and she has seemed never to realize that he carried her to what immortality she will have on this earth. From the point of view of the scholar she committed a sin, too, in losing all Yeats's letters to her. For the reader today Yeats's prophecy that the people of coming days will

> . . . think that you were hard and unkind,
> And blame you with many bitter words,

has come true. Yeats early anticipated what his critics and biographers would say of his love. His friends had already said much on the subject, and his only answer to them was, "None of you understands her force of mind." In his poetry when "He thinks of those who have Spoken Evil of his Beloved," he insisted loyally,

> Their children's children shall say they have lied.

Knowledge of the real Maud Gonne fortifies Yeats's own half realistic, half wildly romantic view of her. "Stubborn with his passion," he sang of her beauty, especially of her beauty of movement, of her charity, of her pride, of her heartlessness, of his friends' dislike of her, of her energy, of her fanaticism. All these things are strictly true. And perhaps the best that can be said of her is that she inspired a great poet to write of her during almost fifty years a cycle of more than sixty poems.

The woman who, next to Maud Gonne, appears most often in Yeats's poetry is Lady Augusta Gregory. The ladies did not like each other, and, characteristically, Maud Gonne has since Lady Gregory's death spitefully attacked her in print. In every way Lady Gregory serves in Yeats's poems as the opposite of

Maud Gonne, for she is kind, calm, tolerant, honorable. In *A Prayer for My Daughter,* Yeats wanted the little girl to grow to be all he thought Lady Gregory was and to be in no way like Maud Gonne. The reasons are clear.

To Yeats, Lady Gregory was not only a dear friend but a symbol of the aristocratic ideal. When he was worn by national struggles and ill from the long strain of hopeless love, Lady Gregory gave him security, comfort, encouragement at Coole. But Yeats's devotion to Coole and its mistress was based more deeply than physical comfort or a liking for an ivory tower where the servants do the living. At Coole he found, he said, intellectual freedom, a place where "men and women are valued for their manhood and their charm, not for their opinions." In Lady Gregory he found also the aristocratic sense of responsibility. She served all about her. Yeats especially approved her tireless devotion to making the Irish ready to rule themselves. She had, he believed, an integrated personality because she was brought up in an aristocratic tradition, with an inherited sense of values. If Yeats generalized too freely in his admiration of the nobility, at Coole and late in life at Penns in the Rocks, the estate of Lady Gerald Wellesley, he found in these two noblewomen a charm, a graciousness he valued highly, and, above all, complete intellectual freedom. In 1909 Yeats wrote, "A great lady is as simple as a good poet. Neither possesses anything that is not ancient and their own, and both are full of uncertainty . . . about all that they merely think." There is no reason to believe that he ever changed this opinion.

To the biographer and critic, Lady Gregory's books, *Our Irish Theatre* and *Hugh Lane,* not only reveal much about Yeats (each volume contains many of his letters) but these books also substantiate the qualities he found in her. Of his poems, *To a House Shaken by the Land Agitation* (the house is Coole, not the House of Lords, as George Moore maliciously pretended to believe), *Nineteen Hundred and Nineteen, Coole Park, Coole and Ballylee,* among others, are, I think, greatly illuminated by knowledge of Lady Gregory and her relation to Yeats through half his lifetime.

When in *The Municipal Gallery Revisited* (*Last Poems*) Yeats summoned his permanent or impermanent images, he devoted most space to Lady Gregory, to Mancini's portrait of her, which Synge praised as the greatest since Rembrandt; and Yeats sadly asked:

> But where is the brush that could show anything
> Of all that pride and that humility?
> And I am in despair that time may bring
> Approved patterns of women or of men
> But not that selfsame excellence again.

Many other poems about Yeats's friends, like the magnificent elegy *In Memory of Major Robert Gregory,* are to us richer if we know more of these friends and of Yeats's relation to them than the surface of the poems can show. Among relatives and friends who appear often are Yeats's grandfather, William Pollexfen, that violent old man who taught his grandson the aristocratic precept, "Only the wasteful virtues earn the sun"; his father, John Butler Yeats, the ideal sire for a poet; his literary friends, Synge and Lionel Johnson; Irish friends of his youth, Standish O'Grady, Eva Gore-Booth, and her sister, Countess Constance Markievicz; and friends who shared his love of the esoteric, Mohini Chatterji, Florence Farr Emery, W. T. Horton, Mac-Gregor Mathers.

The most difficult question in Yeats's life as related to his poetry is his preoccupation with the super-natural, with what he called "that most violent force in history." Yeats early defended to O'Leary his study of magic by saying that the mystical life was the center of all he did, thought, wrote. "It holds to my work," he said, "the same relation that the philosophy of Godwin holds to the work of Shelley . . . the revolt of the soul against the intellect." Early—and indeed late— Yeats pursued the study of magic directly, among Irish peasants, as a member of the Hermetic Society in Dublin, in Madame Blavatsky's séances, in MacGregor Mathers' Order of the Golden Dawn. In all this ex-perimentation, which Yeats has discussed fully in his *Autobiography* and elsewhere, he found symbols and images for poetry; and it is significant that the spirits who, he said, dictated the system he outlined in *A Vision* refused his offer to spend his life in study and elucidation of their teachings. "No," they said, "we have come to give you metaphors for poetry."

Experimentation in séances or the charting of horo-scopes was not enough, and Yeats from youth and especially in maturity pursued an elaborate course of reading to find a kind of philosophic backing for what as poet and, he hoped, inspired seer, he had already envisioned. When some future critic writes Yeats's road to Xanadu (some fragments of this work have been done), he will find a path of reading leading him from Spenser, Shelley, Pater, and Adam's *Axël,* to A. P. Sinnett's *Esoteric Buddhism* and the Christian *Cabala,* from Blake and Swedenborg to Plotinus, Henry More, Vico, Josef Strzygowski, and the *Upanishads,* and ultimately to Swift and Berkeley. Hone says the whole course of Yeats's late reading in philosophy can be traced in the largely unpublished letters to T. E. Sturge Moore.

What is very important to the critic is the fact that Yeats discussed in prose of an autobiographical nature most of the supernatural and philosophical concepts he found in his reading and used in his poetry. Since he was, he insisted, never a scholar and his studies always superficial, he commented with the enthusiasm of a novice on that learning he tried to systematize in *A Vision.* The *Autobiography,* the diaries, especially the recently published *Diary* of 1930, many of the essays, even parts of *A Vision* are intimate revelations of Yeats's feeling and thought. In fact, his friend AE called the introduction to "The Great Wheel," written as a preface to the new edition of *A Vision,* "the most personal of Yeats's writings." As personal revelation, as a record of Yeats's feeling and thought, the critic must, I think, take *A Vision* seriously. Cleanth Brooks and others have already done so; but much work remains in the elucidation of difficult poems by a full group of references to *A Vision* as well as to Yeats's other more or less autobiographical works.

Ego Dominus Tuus is an example of a difficult poem made clear—or at least clearer—by knowledge of Yeats's thought as he revealed it in his far-flung *biographia literaria;* for the poem grew out of Yeats's preoccupation with the supernatural and gathers together several of his basic beliefs. *Ego Dominus Tuus* is of deep significance not only as an embodiment of Yeats's philosophy but because it also involves his whole theory of art and the artist. That Yeats himself thought this poem would need prose elucidation is amply evident. It was published in *Poetry,* October, 1917, and in the same year Yeats used it as a text for exposition in a small volume, *Per Amica Silentia Lunae,* which includes two very personal essays, *Anima Mundi* and *Anima Hominis.* In a letter to his father Yeats called the two essays "An Alphabet," and said they served as a kind of prose backing to his poetry. He repeatedly commented on *Ego Dominus Tuus* in his *Autobiography,* and finally both in the *Autobiography* and in *A Vision* he elaborated his analysis of Dante and Keats, the two poets he considers in the poem.

Ego Dominus Tuus is cast in a dialogue between *Hic* and *Ille,* two parts of the self. The debate between the two embodies Yeats's favorite doctrine that, as he said in *A Vision,* "All things are from antithesis," or, more elaborately, "The whole system [of *A Vision*] is founded upon the belief that ultimate reality, sym-

bolised as the Sphere, falls in human consciousness
. . . into a series of antinomies." Both *Hic* and *Ille*
search for ultimate reality, but their methods are
antithetical. *Hic* seeks to know himself and studies the
works of the great. *Ille* seeks an image and his own opposite; and his search is neither in books nor in himself but somewhere in a world mind or memory. These
antinomies between the specific things sought for
and between the places in which they are sought are
basic to the poem.

Yeats early adopted the old doctrine of *Anima
Mundi,* of a world mind or memory of which a man
may partake, mingling with minds who have followed
a study like his in some other age or in the same age.
Our daily thought is, Yeats said, "but the line of foam
at the shallow edge of a vast luminous sea; Henry
More's *Anima Mundi,* Wordsworth's immortal sea
that brought us hither. . . ." In this vast sea man
searches for reality, for ultimate beauty; and there, according to Yeats, some swim or sail and know all shores.
Hence, at the very beginning of *Ego Dominus Tuus,*
Hic comments that *Ille* has deserted his book, his
tower, his lamp, to stand by the stream in the moon.
(To Yeats the moon is ever the symbol of subjective
life.) Though the best of life has gone, *Ille* is still "En-
thralled by the unconquerable delusion"; he still
traces "Magical shapes." His search is for an inspired, a
supernatural vision from *Anima Mundi.*

In this world mind the poet hopes to find an image
to help him summon his opposite. The all-important

image, Yeats said, must come from above and beyond a man, and he was never sure whether he himself was the seeker or the sought. *Ille,* in the poem, says:

> By the help of an image
> I call to my own opposite, summon all
> That I have handled least, least looked upon.

This opposite, Yeats said repeatedly, is the most difficult thing which is not impossible, because only the greatest difficulty not entirely insurmountable "rouses the will to full intensity." In *A Vision* he wrote on this point: "Only by the pursuit or acceptance of its [the will's] direct opposite, that object of desire or moral ideal which is of all possible things the most difficult, and by forcing that form upon the *Body of Fate* can it [the will] attain self-knowledge and expression." Hence Dante, when in the poem he creates his opposite, sets his chisel to the hardest stone.

Such an image, once found, such an opposite once achieved give to a man the most desired of all states, Unity of Being. The term Unity of Being Yeats said he learned from his father, and he recorded his own unsuccessful search for it in the section of his *Autobiography* called "Hodos Chameliontos," the path of the chameleon. Yeats liked as symbol of this unity Dante's comparison in the *Convito* to a perfectly proportioned human body. Unity of Being, difficult in a heterogeneous age, Yeats said, may yet be found with "a little passion and a little philosophy." In the *Diary* of 1930 he insisted that man can only love Unity of Being, and for that reason conflicts between heterogeneity and unity are conflicts of the whole soul. The modern man, *Hic* in the poem, searches futilely for unity in the mirror, by study of himself, and *Ille* says that thus in recent centuries

> We have lit upon the gentle, sensitive mind
> And lost the old nonchalance of the hand. . . .
> We are but critics, or but half create. . . .

The search for real unity is elsewhere, in *Anima Mundi*.

Involved in this search is Yeats's doctrine of the mask, another element in his belief in the antithetical nature of reality. Active virtue, he said, not the passive acceptance of a code, is "consciously dramatic, the wearing of a mask"; and "all happiness depends on the energy to assume the mask of some other life." If a man cannot imagine and try to assume a mask of a second self, he cannot, according to Yeats, impose discipline upon himself. Such diverse persons as St. Francis and Cesare Borgia made themselves, Yeats thought, "overmastering, creative men by turning from the mirror to meditation upon a mask." But the other self, the antithetical self, can be assumed, Yeats insisted, only by those who are no longer deceived, whose passion is reality.

All these concepts are basic to *Ego Dominus Tuus: Anima Mundi* as an ultimate source of wisdom; the essential image to make clear all a man thinks, feels, is, does; the necessary assumption of a mask of an anti-self; and in all these the search for Unity of Being.

The choice of Dante as the poet who achieved Unity of Being, who found both image and anti-self, Yeats explains fully. The account of Dante is obliquely autobiographical in that Yeats thought of himself as belonging to the same phase in which he placed Dante in his system. In his own search for an image he remembered that place in Dante where he sees in his chamber the Lord of the Terrible Aspect, and seeming to rejoice inwardly at the marvel, he heard many things, but understood few, of these this: *Ego Dominus Tuus.* Dante, Yeats said in *A Vision,* achieved Unity of Being because he had a vision of evil. Yeats believed, too, that only the man who has endured "all imaginable pangs" can create the "greatest imaginable beauty." Dante, Yeats thought, fought a double war: with himself, his own lechery; with his fate, the death of Beatrice, his banishment from Florence. And out of these evils came their opposite: he wrote of the most pure lady poet ever sung and of the divine justice. His mask (not the man Lapo or Guido knew) became the gaunt Dante of the *Divine Comedy.* Disordered, riotous, violently partisan as Dante was as man, as poet, Yeats said, he attained to Unity of Being, as poet he saw all things set in order, had an intellect that served the mask alone, that compelled even those things that opposed it to serve, and was content to see both good and evil. Suffering injustice and the loss of Beatrice, Dante found divine justice and the heavenly Beatrice. The two halves of Dante's nature were so completely joined, according to Yeats, that he seemed to labor for his objects, and yet to desire whatever happened, to be "at the same instant predestinate and free, creation's very self." Dante understood that "fate wrecked what life could not rebuild," had no kind of optimism, had a complete vision of evil; and he found and created a "beauty instinct with terror." Of him *Ille* says in the poem:

> I think he fashioned from his opposite
> An image that might have been a stony face
> Staring upon a Bedouin's horse-hair roof
> From doored and windowed cliff, or half upturned
> Among the coarse grass and the camel-dung.
> He set his chisel to the hardest stone.
> Being mocked by Guido for his lecherous life,
> Derided and deriding, driven out
> To climb that stair and eat that bitter bread,
> He found the unpersuadable justice, he found
> The most exalted lady loved by man.

In the modern world, Yeats said, art is largely given over to propaganda or traditional doctrine.

> For those that love the world serve it in action,
> Grow rich, popular and full of influence,
> And should they paint or write, still it is action:
> The struggle of the fly in marmalade.
> The rhetorician would deceive his neighbours,
> The sentimentalist himself; while art
> Is but a vision of reality.

The real artist, Yeats said, is concerned with those images and regions in his mind that "grow in beauty as they grow in sterility," and can take no part in such action. The islands of loveliness created by pure poets are separated from all the general purposes of life. Yeats found such islands in a few passages in Spenser and not again till Keats's *Endymion*. To such pure poets, Yeats asked, what can the Christian confessor say except "Cease to be artist; cease to be poet"? Yeats

names in his *Autobiography* Ernest Dowson and
Lionel Johnson when he quotes *Ille's* question from
Ego Dominus Tuus:

> What portion in the world can the artist have
> Who has awakened from the common dream
> But dissipation and despair?

Hic protests that Keats was deliberately happy,
loved the world. In *A Vision* Yeats cites Keats as the
almost perfect example of the obsessed man, with his
Body of Fate an enforced love of the world. In him
Yeats found intellectual curiosity weakest and thought
disappearing into image. Yeats found, too, in Keats's
poetry at its best scarcely an image whose subjectivity
had not been heightened by its use by many great poets,
painters, sculptors, artificers. Hence *Ille* in the poem
finds Keats's art happy but his mind, his life, the opposite.

In the final passage of *Ego Dominus Tuus,* neither
of the disputants is in any way convinced by the other's
argument. *Hic* warns *Ille* to cease tracing magical
characters on the sands, to learn style by sedentary
toil and imitation of the great masters. But *Ille* again
avows his faith in the image from *Anima Mundi,* in the
anti-self, who by magic symbols will disclose all he
seeks, will lead him to Unity of Being:

> I call to the mysterious one who yet
> Shall walk the wet sands by the edge of the stream
> And look most like me, being indeed my double,
> And prove of all imaginable things
> The most unlike, being my anti-self,
> And standing by these characters disclose

All that I seek; and whisper it as though
He were afraid the birds, who cry aloud
Their momentary cries before it is dawn,
Would carry it away to blasphemous men.

Blasphemous men, because Yeats dealt with what was to him both philosophy and religion.

These are but a few examples of the ideas, the mysterious, even magical symbols that play a considerable part in Yeats's verse. Edmund Wilson said that they "have little more objective reality than the images of Mallarmé," that they are "the elements and moods of Yeats' complex sensibility." But he adds, "They constitute a world of which one can to some extent get the hang. . . ." Critics of Yeats must take this world into account, for unless they are readers of very rare insight and range, they will need the history of Yeats's thought and feeling, which he took great pains to write down, as a constant guide on their way. Yeats invited us to use this history, even in the interpretation of the early poems based in Irish myths where, he said, "an always personal emotion was woven into a general pattern of myth and symbol." Certainly his philosophic theories gave rise to the plays, which, unrealistic and lyrical as they are, grew directly from his speculations. Several of Yeats's critics have applied his philosophy, founded in myth, to the great poems of Byzantium and the tower, to the poems in which he assumes the mask of Swift; but a full interpretation of the plays in the light of Yeats's philosophy is yet to be made.

Biographical evidence has already been misused in considering Yeats's poems by those critics concerned with Yeats as the literary fop (a phrase made notorious by George Moore's American publisher); or by those critics seriously concerned with Yeats's preoccupation with odors from unknown sources or a green pebble left in a girl's hand at a spiritualistic séance; or, recently most common of all, those critics, like Stephen Spender, much disturbed by what they thought they found to be fascistic in *On the Boiler* and elsewhere. W. H. Auden in his memorial verses to Yeats said, "You were silly like us"; but Auden knew that poetry is not lessened, magnified, or illumined by biographical trivia. Wise and significant use of biographical, especially autobiographical, material to clarify the poems is to be found in the criticism of the contributors whom Mr. Brooks and Mr. Robert Penn Warren summoned to make up the Yeats Memorial Issue of the *Southern Review,* Winter, 1942.

Finally, though one may not naïvely accept all that Yeats says of himself in his *Autobiography* or elsewhere as literal truth, it must always be remembered that he did deliberately furnish for his readers a heavy scaffolding of biographical information. In a peculiar sense, therefore, evidence of this kind is important to the understanding of Yeats's poetry in the ways I have tried to suggest. The very intensity and compactness of the poems of the last twenty-five years of his life may have come in part from his dependence on his readers' knowledge of the autobiographical structure he had made and was making. In the Preface to the privately printed version of *A Vision* (1925) he remarked that having written the book he could find in his poetry the simplicity he had previously sought in vain, that he need no longer write poems like "The Phases of the Moon" or *Ego Dominus Tuus*. Is a poet aesthetically justified in wanting us, expecting us, to know much of his life and thought as a frame for his poetry? Yeats made this assumption and furnished a welter of material for our study. On at least one occasion he scorned scholars as "Bald heads forgetful of their sins," who "cough in ink to the world's end"; but he deliberately left to them a vast deal of work.

PART II

The Methods of Literary Studies

Introduction

༜

By ARTHUR M. MIZENER

THE SYMPOSIUM on the methods of literary studies which follows was originally planned because it seemed a possibility. It looked, that is, as if the various groups which profess an interest in literature had arrived at a point where they could again give something more than a merely nominal recognition to each other. If that kind of grudging respect which demonstrates itself as marked politeness and is the evidence of a healthy state of affairs was once more possible among professors of literature with different specialties, it seemed worth demonstrating, for this possibility has not always existed in the recent past.

This group of papers seems to me to demonstrate the recognition of a unity of purpose among such professors even more dramatically than might have been expected. So alike, indeed, are the arguments by which Mr. Wellek and Mr. Brooks show the interdependence of criticism and literary history that, did I not know better, I should suspect them of collusion. Nor would one anticipate in a textual scholar so sharp a sense of

the closeness of his work to theirs as is represented by
Mr. McAdam's interest in such substantial fact as that
"thirty-three changes" in the revision of *Laon and
Cythna* "soften the sharp atheistical tone." In the same
way, Mr. Downer's awareness that "a knowledge of
theatrical conventions" helps us to make "a surer estimate of a playwright's work"—and perhaps a little,
too, his ability to see a kind of poetry in Mr. Dangle—
makes him a party to the conspiracy. Perhaps it is because these papers are so good in their various kinds
that they show such a happy community of purpose.
But perhaps, too, it is because each kind of literary
studies has once more reached the point where it is
willing honestly to admit its dependence on all the
others.

Six Types of Literary History

❧

By RENÉ WELLEK

THE TERM "literary history" is used today in so many different senses that no intelligent discussion of the issues is possible without clearly conceiving of the various senses the word has borne. I thus shall begin with a sketchy essay in semantics which will, I hope, also outline the main ideas which have determined the writing of "literary history."

During the Renaissance and in the seventeenth century, *historia litteraria* was used to refer to any catalogue of writers or books. The first book by an Englishman to carry the word on the title-page, William Cave's *Scriptorum Ecclesiasticorum Historia Literaria* (London, 1688), is simply a catalogue of theological writers. This earliest conception of "literary history" still survives in our universities in the application of the term to almost any work concerned with books of the more remote past.

The term assumed a more ambitious meaning in Bacon's well-known proposal to write "literary history." [1] He was thinking, of course, not of a history of poetry and imaginative literature but rather of a history of learning, an intellectual history which would include jurisprudence, mathematics, rhetoric, and philosophy. Bacon's proposal was carried out by Henry Hallam in his *Introduction to the Literary History of the Fifteenth, Sixteenth and Seventeenth Centuries* (1837–39). Hallam discusses books on theology, logic, jurisprudence, and mathematics, together with poetry and drama. "Literary history" is conceived of as a history of ideas, in practice as a history of the revival of classical antiquity and of the spread of enlightenment. Bacon and Hallam could be claimed as the forerunners of those many modern "literary historians" who cultivate the history of scholarship or scientific and political thought.

"Literary history" was given a new meaning during the Romantic age. With the growth of romantic nationalism, especially in Germany, "literary history" became a total science of a specific culture, of classical or early Teutonic civilization. Its purpose became the establishment and tracing of a "national spirit," of national ideals and ideologies. In Germany, the brothers Schlegel and the classical philologist Boekh formulated the view very clearly and it soon also penetrated to England. As early as 1831 Carlyle proclaimed this ideal: "The history of a nation's poetry is the essence of its history, political, scientific, religious. The Historian of Poetry has to record the highest aim of a

[1] In *Advancement of Learning* and, with important additions, in *De Augmentis Scientiarum*. See *Works*, ed. J. Spedding, Ellis, *et al.*, III (London, 1857), 329; I, 502–4.

nation, in its successive directions and developments; for by this the Poetry of the nation modulates itself; this is the Poetry of the nation." [2]

Most nineteenth century histories of English literature were written with some such conception in mind. Henry Morley and W. J. Courthope, very different though they were in critical attitude, share the assumption that literature is a document for the study of "national growth" or the "continuous growth of our [English] national institutions." [3] In this country such a view was expounded by Edwin Greenlaw in his *Province of Literary History*.[4] He argues that nothing related to the history of civilization is beyond our province and that literary historians are not "limited to *belles lettres* or even to printed or manuscript records." [5] They should also study painting, music, or archeological evidence. According to Greenlaw's theory, and in the practice of many "literary historians," literary history has thus become not merely closely related to the "history of civilization" but indeed identical with it.

After the romantic age, under the influence of positivism, and of the prestige of the natural sciences, yet another conception of "literary history" began to prevail. "Literary history" was conceived of as a science

[2] In a review of William Taylor's of Norwich *Historic Survey of German Poetry*, reprinted in *Miscellanies* (Centenary ed., New York, 1899), II, 341–42.

[3] Henry Morley, *English Writers: the Writers before Chaucer* (London, 1864), Preface; W. J. Courthope, *A History of English Poetry* (London, 1895), I, xv.

[4] Baltimore, 1931. Johns Hopkins Monographs in Literary History, I.

[5] *Ibid.*, pp. 29, 174.

which was to explain literature in terms of its setting, in terms of antecedent causes. Introducing the term "moment" in his famous triad of *race, milieu* and *moment* Hippolyte Taine took particular account of the historical factors in the determination of literary change; but in most literary historians of this persuasion, the "causal" or "genetic" method disregarding temporal conceptions is central. Sir Sidney Lee has formulated the theory in his inaugural at the University of London. "In literary history," he said "we seek the external circumstances—political, social, economic—in which literature is produced." [6] Most deterministic methods, whether sociological like the Marxist, or psychological like psychoanalysis, should be classed with this conception of "literary history."

Towards the end of the nineteenth century a new conception of "literary history" emerged as a consequence of increasing relativism and "historicism." The view then prevailed that "literary history" is distinguished mainly by absolute "objectivity," by its acceptance of the standards of other ages, by its attempt to enter imaginatively into the mind and attitudes of bygone periods, by its refusal to judge and criticize. In its most general form this point of view could be called the "historical sense": the consciousness that we live at a particular time in history, that men have changed profoundly in the course of history, and that different periods have their own distinct individualities. The rise of the historical sense has been studied with

[6] *The Place of English Literature in the Modern University* (London, 1913), reprinted in *Elizabethan and Other Essays* (London, 1929), p. 7.

some care in Germany by Meinecke and others. It became apparently very vivid only in the later eighteenth century and was important for the rise of the conception of the "national" spirit. But in a radical form as a theory of "historism" it was formulated only in late nineteenth-century Germany.

It seems now to have penetrated directly or indirectly into the United States; and to it, many of our "literary historians" more or less clearly profess allegiance. Hardin Craig, for instance, said recently that the newest and best phase of literary scholarship is the "avoidance of anachronistic thinking." [7] E. E. Stoll, who tries to reconstruct the conventions of the Elizabethan stage and the expectations of its audience, bases his work on the theory that the reconstruction of the original intention of the author is the central task of literary history.[8] Some such theory is implied in the many attempts to study Elizabethan psychological theories, such as the doctrine of humors, or of the scientific or pseudoscientific conceptions of poets.[9] Rosemond Tuve has tried to explain the origin and meaning of metaphysical imagery by reference to the training in Ramean logic received by Donne and his

[7] *Literary Study and the Scholarly Profession* (Seattle, Wash., 1944), p. 70. Cf. also: "The last generation has rather unexpectedly decided that it will discover the meaning and values of old authors themselves and has pinned its faith to the idea, for example, that Shakespeare's own meaning is the greatest of Shakespearean meanings" (pp. 126–27).
[8] E.g., *Poets and Playwrights* (Minneapolis, 1930), p. 217; *From Shakespeare to Joyce* (Garden City, N.Y., 1944), p. ix.; etc.
[9] E.g., in Lily Campbell, *Shakespeare's Tragic Heroes: Slaves of Passion* (Cambridge, 1930); Oscar J. Campbell, "What Is the Matter with Hamlet?" *Yale Review*, XXXII (1942), 309–22. Stoll, who holds to a different variety of historism, attacks this view, e.g., in "Jaques, and the Antiquaries" in *From Shakespeare to Joyce*, pp. 138–45.

contemporaries.[10] As such studies cannot but con-
vince us that different periods had entertained different critical conceptions and conventions, it has been
concluded that each age is a self-contained unity with
its own type of poetry, incommensurate with any
other. This view has been persuasively and candidly
expounded by Frederick Pottle in his *Idiom of
Poetry*.[11] His exposition of such a critical relativism
is the more valuable as he combines it with an acceptance of absolute standards in ethics and religion.

Finally, there is another rather narrow and special
conception of literary history. I allude to the view that
there is an internal development of literature, that
literature has its own history, and that this history can
be written in comparative isolation from that of the
social conditions under which literature was produced. The literary historian in this sense has a task
analogous to that of the historian of art or of music,
who can trace the evolution of portrait painting or of
the sonata without necessarily paying much attention
to the biographies of painters or composers or to the
audience for which the paintings and compositions
were designed. There is such a problem as that of the
change, the development, the continuity of the art of
literature. The conception arose in connection with
Hegelian dialectics and was then modified by nineteenth-century evolutionism. It has been again revived
on the analogy of Wölfflin's history of art in twentieth-
century Germany and, in more Hegelian terms, by the

---

[10] "Imagery and Logic: Ramus and Metaphysical Poetics," *Journal
of the History of Ideas,* III (1942), 365–400.
[11] Ithaca, N.Y., 1941.

Russian formalists. Today, at least in England and the United States, there seems to be almost no consciousness of this problem. "Literary History" in this sense is almost nonexistent. If we ignore the books labeled "literary history," which are such only by courtesy of the bookbinder, we can hardly think of any attempt to write the history of English literature which shows any awareness of the problems involved. Even so prominent a scholar as Sir Herbert Grierson has produced a book called *A Critical History of English Poetry* evincing no grasp of the continuity and internal development of literature and scarcely any awareness of the very existence of these problems.[12]

We have thus distinguished six meanings of the term "literary history": literary history as a 1) history of books; as 2) intellectual history; as the 3) history of national civilizations; as 4) sociological method; as 5) historical relativism; and, finally, as an 6) internal history of literary development. Only now can we criticize these conceptions intelligibly and intelligently.

The first use of "literary history" as an omnibus term for any kind of research into the past is objectionable since there seems no point in giving the name to a piece of textual criticism, editing, a discussion of authorship, of a source, or the like. Obviously, the same methods can be used for purely contemporary material. The term "history" obscures the fact that there is no real distinction between the treatment of the present age and the distant past, that there is nothing particularly "historical" or "literary" about

12 Oxford, 1944, and New York, 1946. For full substantiation see my review in *Western Review* (in press).

much of this work. Such a use is parallel to that of "natural history," which is still, I believe, employed for any description of a plant or animal.

The use of "literary history" for what, in effect, is history of ideas is also misleading. "Literature" here means printed matter. The history of ideas, intellectual history, is a great and worthy subject, possibly more important than the history of literature. But it is a distinct subject with its own methods and criteria, which should not be called "literary history." This is not merely a terminological question. The history of ideas will necessarily impose its own standards of relevance on the material it treats. And then imaginative literature must appear, as A. O. Lovejoy has called it, the "history of ideas in dilution." [13] Poetry as art will seem either insignificant or merely a troublesome and superfluous wrapper for the ideas. Extraneous non-literary criteria will be introduced into literary study and literature will be judged valuable only so far as it yields results for this neighboring discipline.

The same type of criticism must, a fortiori, be applied to the use of literature in a general history of civilization or of a national mind. Literature is used there only as a document, as a symptom of something else. The criteria of value are unliterary; works will and must be judged only on the basis of whether and how far they embody national ideals. Journalistic and rhetorical prose will then frequently deserve preference over great literature as expressing more clearly the "national spirit" or the spirit of a time.

[13] *The Great Chain of Being* (Cambridge, Mass., 1936), p. iv.

The whole use of literature as a document in the history of civilization leads to the extremely difficult and controversial questions of the relation of literature and life, literature and society. How far can literature be considered a reliable document for cultural history? Should not we recognize the obliqueness of the relationship between literature and life, the difficulties and dangers of confusing literature with documents, the specific nature of a fictional statement? Even an apparently realistic novel, the very "slice of life" of the modern naturalist, is actually constructed on certain artistic conventions. The distinctions between romantic and realistic novels are, at least in part, distinctions of mere conventional artistic techniques. The realistic author prefers a type of causation and motivation which strikes us as more probable and lifelike than that of his romantic ancestor, whose devices, such as soliloquy, eavesdropping, and chance meetings, the realistic author will avoid. But the most radical naturalist replaces these devices by conventions of his own. In a later historical perspective we see how similar are the naturalistic novels in choice of theme, type of characterization, nature of events selected or admitted, way of conducting dialogue, and the like, although in their time each was understood to mirror life in a way somehow quite independent of literary tradition.

Still, these observations do not dispose of the very real problem of the relation between literature and life, literature and society. They only point to the extreme dangers of a historical method which treats a work of art as a document. The political historian rightly considers a charter, a treaty, or a diplomatic report as raw material which he has to interpret in order to reconstruct the actual series of events which lie behind these documents. But the literary student can argue that a work of literature is not a document in the historian's sense. The work itself is the directly accessible event of literary history. However much interpretation the work may need, there is no need of reconstructing anything behind it. The historian has to reconstruct the actual happenings (for example, the course of the battle of Waterloo, of a series of diplomatic negotiations, of an institutional change) by accumulating evidence from written documents and by eyewitnesses. The battle of Waterloo is passed beyond recovery; we can only reconstruct its course by inference and can describe its causes and consequences. But it is different with a work of art. The legitimate methods of the historian cannot be transferred mechanically. The work of art is still here: it is open for inspection, it is in itself the subject of literary study; and biographical documents, pronouncements in letters and memoirs, are at most a commentary which may throw light on it but which is not part of the work itself. Without doubt, literature can be used as source material for almost any kind of study, even for the history of medicine or law; but it should be recognized that this is a different type of study with different aims, criteria, and standards.

The sociological method, with its many attempts to explain literature in terms of its setting, is the scientifically most respectable and most valuable of the methods of literary study developed in the nineteenth century. It would be impossible to deny that much light has been thrown on literature by a proper knowledge of the conditions under which it was produced. A much fuller discussion would be needed to differentiate between these causal methods; but I should like to point here to its obvious dangers and limitations. The "fallacy of origins" has been widely discussed and recognized in recent decades. It is clear that mere "genetic," causal study cannot dispose of problems of description, analysis, and evaluation of an object. Causal explanation has its peculiar dangers in literary study. It usually singles out only one kind of external relationship, either psychological or social, and assumes that the work of literature can be completely reduced to being the consequences of these outside forces. Becoming thus either an illustration or a symptom of a state of mind or a social situation, the work is ignored in its actual essence and integrity. But literature has its own independent life, itself influences society, is not merely a mirror of an author's mind or of the play of social forces. The causal method forgets literary convention and tradition and disintegrates the individual work of art.

The type of "literary history" I have called historical relativism is also open to grave objections. At its finest, the method requires an effort of imagination, of empathy, or deep congeniality with a bygone age or a vanished taste. Indubitably successful efforts have been made to reconstruct the general outlook on life,

the attitudes, conceptions, prejudices, and underlying assumptions of the different civilizations. We
know a great deal about the Greek attitude towards
the gods or women and slaves; we can describe the
cosmology of the Middle Ages in detail; and we have
attempted to show the very different manner of seeing, or at least the very different artistic traditions and
conventions underlying, Byzantine and Chinese art.
In the study of literature, this attempt at historical
reconstruction leads to great stress on the intentions
of the artist, which it is assumed can be studied in the
history of criticism and sensibility. Underlying much
study of this sort is the theory that the only and true
meaning of a work of art is in the intention of the
author. It is usually assumed that if we can ascertain
this intention and can see that the author has fulfilled
it we have also disposed of the problem of value. The
author has fulfilled a contemporary aesthetic purpose,
and there is no longer any need or even any possibility
of criticizing his work. The method thus leads to complete relativism, to an anarchy, or rather leveling, of all
values. Only one standard remains: that of contemporary success. There are then not one or two but
literally hundreds of independent, diverse, and mutually exclusive conceptions of literature, each of
which is in some way "right." The ideal of poetry is
broken up in so many splinters that nothing remains
of it. Its extreme form is the Chicago Neo-Aristotelian-
ism which denies the possibility of a general theory of
literature and leaves us with unique and thus incommensurate and equal works. A more moderate form is

the view that there are polar poetical ideas which are so different that there is no common denominator between them: Classicism and Romanticism, the ideal of Pope and Wordsworth.

The method can be criticized with convincing arguments which destroy its very presuppositions. The whole idea that the "intention" of the author is the proper subject of literary history seems quite mistaken.[14] Let me pass over the difficulty and even impossibility of reconstructing the intentions of an author when we have no contemporary evidence, no explicit profession or when we have to deal with precritical times. Even if we know the "intentions" we must never forget that they are a posteriori ratiocinations, commentaries which may go far beyond the finished work of art or may be far below or far aside the mark. Divergence between intention and actual performance is a common phenomenon in the history of literature. The meaning of a work of art is not exhausted or even equivalent to its intention. Its system of values leads an independent life; it becomes completely dissociated from the mental processes of its original author and goes itself through a long historical process.

The total meaning of a work of art cannot be defined merely in terms of its meaning for the author and his contemporaries. It is rather the result of a process of

[14] A fuller development of this point is this writer's "The Mode of Existence of a Literary Work of Art," *Southern Review,* VII (1942), 735–54. See also W. K. Wimsatt, Jr., and M. C. Beardsley, "Intention," in *Dictionary of World Literature,* ed. Joseph E. Shipley (New York, 1944), pp. 326–29, and "The Intentional Fallacy," *Sewanee Review,* LIV (1946), 468–88.

accretion; a result of the history of its criticism by its many readers. It seems unnecessary and actually impossible to declare, as the historical reconstructionists do, that this whole process is irrelevant and that we must return only to its beginning.[15] It is simply not possible to cease to be a man of the twentieth century while one engages in a judgment of the past: we cannot forget the associations of our own language, the newly acquired attitudes, the impact and import of the last centuries. We cannot become a contemporary reader of Homer or Chaucer or a member of the audience of the *Globe*. Even if we should make an effort in this direction we would always hold our modern consciousness in suspense. If we were really able to reconstruct the meaning which *Hamlet* held for its contemporary audience we would merely impoverish its meaning. We would suppress the legitimate meanings which later generations found in *Hamlet*. Nor is it sufficient (at least for the historical scholar) to judge a work of art merely from the point of view of our own time. It is not even clear why this or that time should be superior to any other and why it might not be instructive to look at a work of art from the point of view of a third time, neither contemporaneous with us or with the author.

In practice, of course, such clear-cut choices are scarcely feasible. We must simply beware of both false

[15] See Louis Teeter, "Scholarship and the Art of Criticism," *ELH*, V (1938), 173–194; Harold Cherniss, "The Biographical Fashion in Literary Criticism," *University of California Publications in Classical Philology*, XII (1943), 279–92. E.g., "What reason could there be for studying a work which had no meaning except for a single audience in a single spot at a single moment of the past?" (p. 289).

relativism and false absolutism. Values grow out of the historical process of valuation, which they in turn help make us understand. The answer to historical relativism is not a frozen doctrinaire absolutism which denies the reality of historical change by slogans like the "sameness of human nature" or the "universality of art." We must rather adopt a view for which I have borrowed the term "perspectivism" from Ortega y Gasset: we must be able to refer a work of art to the values of its own time and of all the periods subsequent to its own, convinced as we are that a work of art is both "eternal" (that is, preserves a certain identity) and "historical" (that is, passes through a process of development which can be traced). Relativism reduces the history of literature to a series of discrete and hence finally incomprehensible and mutually exclusive fragments, while most absolutisms serve either only a passing present-day situation or are based like the standards of the Neo-Humanists, on some abstract ideal which is unjust to the historical variety of poetry. Perspectivism means that we recognize that there is one poetry, one literature, comparable in all ages, developing, changing, full of possibilities. Literature is neither a series of unique works with nothing in common nor a series of works enclosed in time-cycles of Romanticism or Classicism, nor is it, of course, the "block-universe" of sameness and immutability an older Classicism thought of as ideal. Both absolutism and relativism are false, but today the more insidious danger, at least in America, is a relativism leading to an anarchy of values, to a surrender of the task of criticism.

The last conception of literary history, that of an internal history of art, is nearest to the specific task of the literary student. Having expounded its merits and difficulties elsewhere,[16] I am ashamed to rehearse again the arguments for it. Whatever the difficulties attendant on the concept of literary development, such internal history is a challenge to the literary student. It is not a Utopian speculative scheme: it has been practised more or less consciously, with more or less clearly defined criteria, by everyone who has tried to write the history of a genre such as the drama, or of an individual factor of a work of art such as the history of the artistic development of a single author, of a period and, of course, of a national literature, and ultimately of world literature. There is nothing discouraging in the fact that "literary history" has a future as well as a past, a future which does not consist merely in the filling of gaps and the correction of the mistakes of our predecessors. The conception of literary history can be criticized as unduly purist in its emphasis on the internal history of literature. But this concentration seems at the very least a useful antidote to the expansionist movement in which literary history has lost all specific meaning.

Now that we have surveyed and criticized the different conceptions of "literary history," it will be easy to define the relation between literary history and criticism, a relation which has excited much debate

[16] "The Theory of Literary History" in *Travaux du cercle linguistique de Prague*, VI (1936), 173–92, and "Literary History" in *Literary Scholarship: Its Aims and Methods*, ed. Norman Foerster (Chapel Hill, N.C., 1941), pp. 91–130.

and is still a burning issue in our universities. There is no use, I think, in denying that there is a conflict. A scholar who is interested in criticism, in a centrally literary study, must reject as alien to his purposes the "literary history" which is either a history of ideas or the history of a national spirit. All these are legitimate subjects in which, however, literature is used as a document in the study of something else. The literary critic must also reject historical relativism, since it denies the function of the critic and ends in an anarchy of values. The literary critic will, however, profit greatly from the sociological method, from all attempts to shed light on the work of literature by a study of its setting. But while he will recognize the exegetical value of much historical study he must decline to go all the way with those who would study literature in causal terms. While literature is in constant relationships with other activities of man, it has its own specific character and function and its own development which is irreducible to any other activity. Otherwise, it would cease to be literature and lose its reason for existence: it would become second-rate philosophy, religion, ethics, or even propaganda or an anodyne in Richardsian mental therapy. Unfortunately, because of his healthy distrust of historical relativism and general cultural history, the literary critic has often been led to reject the historical method *in toto*. Many literary critics ignore the very real problem of history and do not see that an internal history of literature is an important part of all literary study.

There is simply no conflict or contradiction between literary criticism and literary history in this last sense. Literary history is necessary for the critic if he does not want to go constantly astray in his judgments. Without literary history, the critic could not know which work is original and which derivative. He would constantly blunder through his ignorance of historical conditions in his understanding of specific works of art. The critic possessed of little or no history is inclined to make careless guesses or to indulge in autobiographical "adventures among masterpieces," and, on the whole, will avoid concern with the more remote past, content to hand that over to the antiquary or the "philologist."

But, conversely, no literary history (at least in our last sense) is possible without criticism. There have been attempts to isolate literary history from theory and criticism. For example F. W. Bateson argues that literary history shows A to derive from B, while criticism pronounces A to be better than B. The first type according to this view, deals with verifiable facts; the second with matters of opinion which imply an element of faith on the reader's part.[17] But this distinction is quite untenable. There are simply no data in literary history which are completely neutral "facts." Value-judgments are implied in the very choice of materials; in the simple preliminary distinction between books and literature, in the mere allocation of space to this or that author. Even the ascertaining of a date or a title presupposes some kind of judgment—one which selects this particular book or event from millions of

[17] "Correspondence" in answer to F. R. Leavis's criticism of Bateson's *English Poetry and the English Language* in *Scrutiny*, IV (1935), 181.

other books or events. Even if we grant that certain facts are comparatively neutral, facts such as dates, titles, biographical events, we grant merely that some kinds of annals of literature can be compiled. But any question a little more advanced, even of textual criticism or of sources and influences, requires constant acts of judgment. Such an apparently neutral and objective statement as "Pope derives from Dryden" presupposes not only the act of selecting Dryden and Pope out of the innumerable versifiers of their times, but requires a knowledge of the characteristics of Dryden and Pope and a constant activity of weighing, comparing, and selecting, which is essentially critical. The question of the collaboration of Beaumont and Fletcher is insoluble unless we accept the important principle that certain stylistic devices are related to one rather than to the other of the two writers. In practice, no literary history has ever been written without some principles of selection and some attempt at characterization and evaluation. Literary historians who deny the importance of criticism are themselves unconscious critics, usually derivative critics, who have merely taken over traditional standards and reputations. Usually, today, they are belated Romanticists who have closed their minds to all other types of art and especially to more recent literature. But, as the English philosopher R. F. Collingwood has said very pertinently, a man "who claims to know that Shakespeare is a poet is tacitly claiming to know whether Miss Stein is a poet and if not, why not." [18]

The whole supposed exemption of the literary his-

[18] *The Principles of Art* (Oxford, 1938), p. 4.

torian from any need of criticism and theory is false and that for a simple reason: every work of art is directly accessible to observation and is a solution of certain artistic problems, whether it was composed yesterday or a thousand years ago. It cannot be analyzed, characterized, and evaluated without constant recourse to critical principles. "The literary historian," we conclude with Norman Foerster, "must be a critic in order to be a proper historian." [19]

[19] *The American Scholar* (Chapel Hill, N.C., 1929).

Literary Criticism

≯

By CLEANTH BROOKS

THE EASIEST ERROR into which we may fall in defin-
ing the relationship between historical and critical
studies is illustrated by the preface of Maurice Kelley's
interesting book on Milton, *This Great Argument.*
For Kelley, the problem of exegesis is almost amus-
ingly simple: we will read Milton's *Christian Doctrine*
to find out what Milton's ideas are, and then we shall
be able to understand his *Paradise Lost,* explaining the
tangled and difficult poetic document by means of the
explicit prose statement. But Kelley's argument rests
not only upon the assumption that the Milton who
wrote the *Christian Doctrine* was precisely and at all
points the same man who composed *Paradise Lost*—a
matter which, for all practical purposes, may well be
true; it rests upon the further and much more dangerous assumption that Milton was able to *say* in *Paradise Lost* exactly what he intended to say; and that
what he supposed he had put into that poem is actually
to be found there. In short, Mr. Kelley tends to make
the assumption about poetry which most of us con-

stantly make; namely, that a poem is essentially a decorated and beautified piece of prose.

But I propose to deal here with a more modest example than Milton's epic. I propose to illustrate from Marvell's "Horatian Ode." If we follow the orthodox procedure, the obvious way to understand the "Ode" is to ascertain by historical evidence—by letters and documents of all kinds—what Marvell really thought of Cromwell, or, since Marvell apparently thought different things of Cromwell at different times, to ascertain the date of the "Ode," and then neatly fit it into the particular stage of Marvell's developing opinion of Cromwell. But this is at best a relatively coarse method which can hope to give no more than a rough approximation of the poem; and there lurk in it some positive perils. For to ascertain what Marvell the man thought of Cromwell, and even to ascertain what Marvell as poet consciously intended to say in his poem, will not prove that the poem actually says this, or all this, or merely this. This last remark, in my opinion, does not imply too metaphysical a notion of the structure of a poem. There is surely a sense in which any one must agree that a poem has a life of its own, and a sense in which it provides in itself the only criterion by which what it says can be judged. It is a commonplace that the poet sometimes writes better than he knows, and, alas, on occasion, writes worse than he knows. The history of English literature will furnish plenty of examples of both cases.

As a matter of fact, Marvell's "Ode" is not a shockingly special case. Indeed, I have chosen it for my example, not because it is special—not because I hope to reveal triumphantly that what it really says is something quite opposed to what we have supposed it to be saying—but because it seems to me a good instance of the normal state of affairs. Yet, even so, the "Ode" will provide us with problems enough. To the scholar who relies upon the conventional approach, the problems become rather distressingly complicated.

Let us review the situation briefly. Hard upon his composition of the "Ode" in 1650, Marvell had published in 1649 a poem "To his Noble Friend, Mr. Richard Lovelace," and a poem "Upon the Death of the Lord Hastings." Both Margoliouth and Legouis find these poems rather pro-Royalist in sentiment and certainly it is difficult to read them otherwise. If we add to these poems the "Elegy upon the Death of My Lord Francis Villiers," a Cavalier who was killed fighting for the King in 1649, the Royalist bias becomes perfectly explicit. As Margoliouth puts it: "If [the elegy on Villiers] is Marvell's, it is his one unequivocal royalist utterance; it throws into strong relief the transitional character of *An Horatian Ode* where royalist principles and admiration for Cromwell the Great Man exist side by side. . . ."

A transition in views there must have been, but the transition certainly cannot be graphed as a steadily rising curve when we take into account Marvell's next poem, "Tom May's Death." May died in November, 1650. Thus we have the "Horatian Ode," which was almost certainly written in the summer of 1650, preceding by only a few months a poem in which Marvell seems to slur at the Commander of the Parliamentary armies—either Essex or Fairfax—as "Spartacus," and to reprehend May himself as a renegade poet who has prostituted the mystery of the true poets. The curve of Marvell's political development shows still another surprising quirk when we recall that only a few months after his attack on May, Marvell was to be living under Spartacus Fairfax's roof, acting as tutor to his little daughter Mary.

Let me interrupt this summary to say that I am not forcing the evidence so as to crowd the historian into the narrowest and most uncomfortable corner possible. On the contrary, whatever forcing of the evidence has been done has been done by the editors and the historians. If we limit ourselves to historical evidence, it is possible to suppose that "Tom May's Death" was actually written on the Hill at Billborrow; and Margoliouth chooses early 1651 as the probable date for Marvell's arrival at Appleton House only because, as he says, " 'Tom May's Death' is not the sort of poem Marvell would have written under Fairfax's roof."

There is no need, in view of our purposes, to extend the review of Marvell's political development through the late 1650's with their Cromwellian poems or through the Restoration period with its vexed problems concerning which of the anti-court satires are truly, and which are falsely, ascribed to Marvell. The problem of Marvell's attitude through the years 1649–51 will provide sufficient scope for this examination of some of the relations and interrelations of the historical approach and the critical approach. For there is still another complication, which has received less attention than it deserves. It is the curious fact that the "Horatian Ode" in which Marvell seems to affirm the ancient rights of the monarchy—

> Though Justice against Fate complain,
> And plead the antient Rights in vain—

is full of echoes of the poetry of Tom May, the poet whom Marvell was, a few months later, to denounce for having failed poetry in the hour of crisis:

> When the Sword glitters ore the Judges head,
> And fear the Coward Churchmen silenced,
> Then is the Poets time, 'tis then he drawes,
> And single fights forsaken Vertues cause.
> He, when the wheel of Empire, whirleth back,
> And though the World's disjointed Axel crack,
> Sings still of *antient Rights* and better Times,
> Seeks wretched good, arraigns successful Crimes.

The echoes of May's poetry, of course, may well have been unconscious: to me it is significant that they are from May's translation of Lucan's poem on the Roman civil wars. (The relevant passage from Margoliouth's notes will be found on pp. 157–58.) I must say that I find the parallels quite convincing and that I am a little surprised at Margoliouth's restraint in not pushing his commentary further. For one is tempted to suppose that in the year or so that followed the execution of Charles, Marvell was obsessed with the problem of the poet's function in such a crisis; that the poet May was frequently in his mind through a double connection— through the parallels between the English and the

Roman civil war, Lucan's poem on which May had translated, and through May's conduct as a partisan of the Commonwealth; and that the "Horatian Ode" and "Tom May's Death," though so different in tone, are closely related and come out of the same general state of mind. But to hazard all this is to guess at the circumstances of Marvell's composition of these poems. It can be only a guess, and, in any case, it takes us into a consideration of what must finally be a distinct problem: how the poem came to be; whereas our elected problem is rather: what the poem is. I am, by the way, in entire sympathy with the essay "The Intentional Fallacy," by W. K. Wimsatt and M. C. Beardsley, recently published in *The Sewanee Review*. We had best not try to telescope the separate problems of "the psychology of composition" and that of "objective evaluation." I have no intention of trying to collapse them here.

Well, what is "said" in the "Horatian Ode"? What is the speaker's attitude toward Cromwell and toward Charles? M. Legouis sees in the "Ode" a complete impartiality, an impartiality which is the product of Marvell's nonparticipation in the wars. Legouis can even speak of the poem as "ce monument d'indifférence en matière de régime politique." But the "Ode," though it may be a monument of impartiality, is not a monument of indifference. To read it in this fashion is to miss what seems to me to be a passionate interest in the issues, an interest which is manifested everywhere in the poem. It is true that we have no evidence that Marvell ever served in the civil war, but we had better not leap to conclusions of his indifference from that. My own guess is that some young Cavaliers who shed their blood for the King thought and felt less deeply about the issues than does the speaker of this poem. The tone is not that of a "plague o' both your houses" nor is it that of "the conflict provided glory enough to be shared by both sides."

Mr. Margoliouth comes much closer to the point. He sums up as follows: "The ode is the utterance of a constitutional monarchist, whose sympathies have been with the King, but who yet believes more in men than in parties or principles, and whose hopes are fixed now on Cromwell, seeing in him both the civic ideal of a ruler without personal ambition, and the man of destiny moved by and yet himself driving a power which is above justice." This statement is plausible, and for its purposes, perhaps just. But does it take us very far—even on the level of understanding Marvell the man? What sort of constitutional monarchist is it who "believes more in men than in . . . principles"? Or who can accept a "power which is above justice"? I do not say that such a monarchist cannot exist. My point is that Margoliouth's statement raises more problems than it solves. Furthermore, in what sense are the speaker's hopes "fixed . . . on Cromwell"? And how confident is he that Cromwell is "without personal ambition"? I have quoted earlier Margoliouth's characterization of the "Ode" as a poem "where royalist principles and admiration for Cromwell the Great Man exist side by side." I think that they do exist side by side, but if so, how are they related? Do they exist in separate layers, or are they somehow unified? Unified, in some sense, they must be if the "Ode" is a poem and not a heap of fragments.

I hope that my last statement indicates the kind of question which we finally have to face and answer. It is a problem of poetic organization. As such, it addresses itself properly to the critic. The historical scholars have not answered it, for it is a question which cannot be answered in terms of historical evidence. (This is not to say, of course, that the same man may not be both historical scholar and critic.) Moreover, I have already taken some pains to indicate how heavily the critic, on his part, may need to lean upon the historian. To put the matter into its simplest terms: the critic obviously must know what the words of the poem mean, something which immediately puts him in debt to the linguist; and since many of the words in this poem are proper nouns, in debt to the historian as well. I am not concerned to exalt the critic at the expense of specialists in other disciplines: on the contrary, I am only concerned to show that he has a significant function, and to indicate what the nature of that function is.

But I am not so presumptuous as to promise a solution to the problem. Instead, the reader will have to be content with suggestions—as to what the "Ode" is not saying, as to what the "Ode" may be saying—in short, with explorations of further problems. Many critical problems, of course, I shall have to pass over and some important ones I shall only touch upon. To illustrate:

there is the general Roman cast given to the "Ode."
Marvell has taken care to make no specifically Christian references in the poem. Charles is Caesar; Cromwell is a Hannibal; on the scaffold, Charles refuses to
call with "vulgar spight," not on God, but on "the
Gods," and so on. Or to point to another problem,
metaphors drawn from hunting pervade the poem.
Charles chases himself to Carisbrooke; Cromwell is
like the falcon; Cromwell will soon put his dogs in
"near/The *Caledonian* Deer." Or, to take up the
general organization of the poem: Marvell seems to
have used the celebrated stanzas on Charles's execution to divide the poem into two rather distinct parts:
first, Cromwell's rise to power; and second, Cromwell's
wielding of the supreme power. This scheme of division, by the way, I intend to make use of in the discussion that follows. But I shall try, in general, to limit
it to the specific problem of the speaker's attitude
toward Cromwell, subordinating other critical problems to this one, which is, I maintain, essentially a
critical problem too.

From historical evidence alone we would suppose
that the attitude toward Cromwell in this poem would
have to be a complex one. And this complexity is reflected in the ambiguity of the compliments paid to
him. The ambiguity reveals itself as early as the
second word of the poem. It is the "forward" youth
whose attention the speaker directs to the example
of Cromwell. "Forward" may mean no more than
"high-spirited," "ardent," "properly ambitious"; but
the *New English Dictionary* sanctions the possibility

that there lurks in the word the sense of "presumptuous," "pushing." The forward youth can no longer
now

> in the Shadows sing
> His Numbers languishing.

In the light of Cromwell's career, he must forsake the
shadows and his "Muses dear" and become the man
of action.

The speaker, one observes, does not identify Cromwell himself as the "forward youth," or say directly
that Cromwell's career has been motivated by a striv-
ing for fame. But the implications of the first two
stanzas do carry over to him. There is, for example, the
important word "so" to relate Cromwell to these
stanzas:

> So restless *Cromwel* could not cease. . . .

And "restless" is as ambiguous in its meanings as "forward," and in its darker connotations even more damn-
ing. For, though "restless" can mean "scorning indo-
lence," "willing to forego ease," it can also suggest the
man with a maggot in the brain. "To cease," used in-
transitively, is "to take rest, to be or remain at rest,"
and the *New English Dictionary* gives instances as late
as 1701. Cromwell's "courage high" will not allow him
to rest "in the inglorious Arts of Peace." And this
thirst for glory, merely hinted at here by negatives, is
developed further in the ninth stanza:

> Could by industrious Valour climbe
> To ruine the great Work of Time.

"Climb" certainly connotes a kind of aggressiveness.

In saying this we need not be afraid that we are reading into the word some smack of such modern phrases as "social climber." Marvell's translation of the second chorus of Seneca's *Thyestes* sufficiently attests that the work could have such associations for him:

> Climb at *Court* for me that will
> Tottering favors Pinacle;
> All I seek is to lye still.

Cromwell, on the other hand, does not seek to lie still—has sought something quite other than this. His valor is called—strange collocation—an "industrious valour," and his courage is too high to brook a rival:

> For 'tis all one to Courage high
> The Emulous or Enemy;
> And with such to inclose,
> Is more then to oppose.

The implied metaphor is that of some explosive which does more violence to that which encloses it, the powder to its magazine, for instance, than to some wall which merely opposes it—against which the charge is fired.

But the speaker has been careful to indicate that Cromwell's motivation has to be conceived of as more complex than any mere thirst for glory. He has even pointed this up. The forward youth is referred to as one who "would appear"—that is, as one who wills to leave the shadows of obscurity. But restless Cromwell "could not cease"—for Cromwell it is not a question of will at all, but of a deeper compulsion. Restless Cromwell could not cease, if he would.

Indeed, the lines that follow extend the suggestion

that Cromwell is like an elemental force—with as little will as the lightning bolt, and with as little conscience:

> And, like the three-fork'd Lightning, first
> Breaking the Clouds where it was nurst,
>   Did thorough his own Side
>   His fiery way divide.

We are told that the last two lines refer to Cromwell's struggle after Marston Moor with the leaders of the Parliamentary party. Doubtless they do, and the point is important for our knowledge of the poem. But what is more important is that we be fully alive to the force of the metaphor. The clouds have bred the lightning bolt, but the bolt tears its way through the clouds, and goes on to blast the head of Caesar himself. As Margoliouth puts it: "The lightning is conceived as tearing through the side of his own body the cloud." In terms of the metaphor, then, Cromwell has not spared his own body: there is no reason therefore to be surprised that he has not spared the body of Charles.

I do not believe that I overemphasized the speaker's implication that Cromwell is a natural force. A few lines later the point is reinforced with another naturalistic figure, an analogy taken from physics:

> Nature that hateth emptiness,
> Allows of penetration less:
>   And therefore must make room
>   Where greater Spirits come . . .

The question of right, the imagery insists, is beside the point. If nature will not tolerate a power vacuum, no more will it allow two bodies to occupy the same space. (It is amusing, by the way, that Marvell has boldly introduced into his analogy borrowed from physics the nonphysical term "Spirits"; yet I do not think that the clash destroys the figure. Since twenty thousand angels can dance on the point of a needle, two spirits, even though one of them is a greater spirit, ought to be able to occupy the same room. But two spirits, as Marvell conceives of spirits here, will jostle one another, and one must give way. True, the greater spirit is immaterial, but he is no pale abstraction—he is all air and fire, the "force of angry Heavens flame." The metaphor ought to give less trouble to the reader of our day than it conceivably gave to readers bred up on Newtonian physics.)

What are the implications for Charles? Does the poet mean to imply that Charles has angered heaven—that he has merited his destruction? There is no suggestion that Cromwell is a thunderbolt hurled by an angry Jehovah—or even by an angry Jove. The general emphasis on Cromwell as an elemental force is thoroughly relevant here to counter this possible misreading. Certainly, in the lines that follow there is nothing to suggest that Charles has angered heaven, or that the Justice which complains against his fate is anything less than justice.

I began this examination of the imagery with the question, "What is the speaker's attitude toward Cromwell?" We have seen that the speaker more than once hints at his thirst for glory:

> So restless *Cromwel* could not cease . . .
> Could by industrious Valour climbe . . .

But we have also seen that the imagery tends to view
Cromwell as a natural phenomenon, the bolt bred in
the cloud. Is there a contradiction? I think not. Cromwell's is no vulgar ambition. If his valor is an "industrious Valour," it contains plain valor too of a
kind perfectly capable of being recognized by any
Cavalier:

> What Field of all the Civil Wars,
> Where his were not the deepest Scars?

If the driving force has been a desire for glory, it is a
glory of that kind which allows a man to become dedicated and, in a sense, even selfless in his pursuit of it.
Moreover, the desire for such glory can become so
much a compulsive force that the man does not appear
to act by an exercise of his personal will but seems to
become the very will of something else. There is in
the poem, it seems to me, at least one specific suggestion of this sort:

> But through adventrous War
> Urged his active Star. . . .

Cromwell is the marked man, the man of destiny, but
he is not merely the man governed by his star. Active
though it be, he cannot remain passive, even in relation to it: he is not merely urged by it, but himself
urges it on.

Yet, if thus far Cromwell has been treated as naked
force, something almost too awesome to be considered
as a man, the poet does not forget that after all he is a
man too—that "the force of angry Heavens flame" is
embodied in a human being:

> And, if we would speak true,
> Much to the Man is due.

The stanzas that follow proceed to define and praise that manliness—the strength, the industrious valor, the cunning. (You will notice that I reject the interpretation which would paraphrase "Much to the Man is due" as "After all, Cromwell has accomplished much that is good." Such an interpretation could sort well enough with Legouis's picture of Marvell as the cold and detached honest broker between the factions: unfortunately it will not survive a close scrutiny of the grammar and the general context in which the passage is placed.)

One notices that among the virtues comprising Cromwell's manliness, the speaker mentions his possession of the "wiser art":

> Where, twining subtile fears with hope,
> He wove a Net of such a scope,
>   That *Charles* himselfe might chase
>   To *Caresbrooks* narrow case.

On this point Cromwell has been cleared by all the modern historians (except perhaps Mr. Hilaire Belloc). Charles's flight to Carisbrooke Castle, as it turned out, aided Cromwell, but Cromwell could have hardly known that it would; and there is no evidence that he cunningly induced the King to flee to Carisbrooke. Royalist pamphleteers, of course, believed that Cromwell did, and used the item in their general bill of damnation against Cromwell. How does the speaker use it here—to damn or to praise? We tend to answer, "To praise." But then it behooves us to notice what is being praised. The things praised are Cromwell's talents as such—the tremendous disciplined powers which Cromwell brought to bear against the King.

For the end served by those powers, the speaker has no praise at all. Rather he has gone out of his way to insist that Cromwell was deaf to the complaint of Justice and its pleading of the "antient Rights." The power achieved by Cromwell is a "forced Pow'r"—a usurped power. On this point the speaker is unequivocal. I must question therefore Margoliouth's statement that Marvell sees in Cromwell "the man of destiny moved by . . . a power that is above justice." Above justice, yes, in the sense that power is power and justice is not power. The one does not insure the presence of the other. Charles has no way to vindicate his "helpless Right," but it is no less Right because it is helpless. But the speaker, though he is not a cynic, is a realist. A kingdom cannot be held by mere pleading of the "antient Rights":

> But those do hold or break
> As Men are strong or weak.

In short, the more closely we look at the "Ode," the more clearly apparent it becomes that the speaker has chosen to emphasize Cromwell's virtues as a man, and likewise, those of Charles as a man. The poem does not debate which of the two was right, for that issue is not even in question. In his treatment of Charles, then, the speaker no more than Charles himself attempts to vindicate his "helpless Right." Instead, he emphasizes his dignity, his fortitude, and what has finally to be called his consummate good taste. The portraits of the two men beautifully supplement each other. Cromwell is—to use Aristotle's distinction—the man of character, the man of action, who "does both act and know." Charles, on the other hand, is the man of passion, the man who is acted upon, the man who knows how to suffer. The contrast is pointed up in half a dozen different ways.

Cromwell, acted upon by his star, is not passive but actually urges his star. Charles in "acting"—in chasing away to Carisbrooke—actually is passive—performs the part assigned to him by Cromwell. True, we can read "chase" as an intransitive verb (the *New English Dictionary* sanctions this use for the period): "that Charles himself might hurry to Carisbrooke." But the primary meaning asserts itself in the context: "that Charles might chase himself to Carisbrooke's narrow case." For this hunter, now preparing to lay his dogs in "near/The *Caledonian* Deer," the royal quarry has dutifully chased itself.

Even in the celebrated stanzas on the execution, there is ironic realism as well as admiration. In this fullest presentation of Charles as king, he is the player king, the king acting in a play. He is the "Royal Actor" who knows his assigned part and performs it with dignity. He truly adorned the "Tragick Scaffold"

> While round the armed Bands
> Did clap their bloody hands.

The generally received account is that the soldiers clapped their hands so as to make it impossible for Charles's speech to be heard. But in the context this reference to hand-clapping supports the stage metaphor. What is being applauded? Cromwell's resolution in bringing the King to a deserved death? Or Charles's resolution on the scaffold as he suffered that death? Marvell was too good a poet to resolve the ambiguity. It is enough that he makes the armed bands applaud.

It has not been pointed out, I believe, that Robert Wild, in his poem on "The Death of Mr. Christopher Love," has echoed a pair of Marvell's finest lines. Love was beheaded by Cromwell on August 22, 1651. In Wild's poem, Marvell's lines

> But with his keener Eye
> The Axes edge did try

become: "His keener words did their sharp Ax exceed." The point is of no especial importance except that it indicates, since Wild's poem was evidently written shortly after Love's execution, that in 1651 the "Horatian Ode" was being handed about among the Royalists. For Wild was that strange combination, an English Presbyterian Royalist.

I have pointed out earlier that the second half of the poem begins here with the reference to

> that memorable Hour
> Which first assur'd the forced Pow'r.

Cromwell is now the *de facto* head of the state, and the speaker, as a realist, recognizes that fact. Cromwell is seen henceforth, not primarily in his character as the destroyer of the monarchy, but as the agent of the new state that has been erected upon the dead body of the King. The thunderbolt simile, of the first part of the poem, gives way here to the falcon simile in this second

part of the poem. The latter figure revises and quali-
fies the former: it repeats the suggestion of ruthless
energy and power, but Cromwell falls from the sky
now, not as the thunderbolt, but as the hunting hawk.
The trained falcon is not a wanton destroyer, nor an ir-
responsible one. It knows its master: it is perfectly disciplined:

> She, having kill'd, no more does search,
> But on the next green Bow to pearch . . .

The speaker's admiration for Cromwell the man
culminates, it seems to me, here. Cromwell might
make the Fame his own; he *need* not present kingdoms
to the state. He might assume the crown rather than
crowning each year. Yet he forbears:

> Nor yet grown stiffer with Command,
> But still in the *Republick's* hand . . .

Does the emphasis on "still" mean that the speaker is
surprised that Cromwell has continued to pay homage
to the republic? Does he imply that Cromwell may not
always do so? Perhaps not: the emphasis is upon the
fact that he need not obey and yet does. Yet the compliment derives its full force from the fact that the
homage is not forced, but voluntary and even somewhat unexpected. And a recognition of this point implies the recognition of the possibility that Cromwell
will not always so defer to the commonwealth.

And now what of the republic which Cromwell so
ruthlessly and efficiently serves? What is the speaker's
attitude toward it? To begin with, the speaker recognizes that its foundations rest upon the bleeding head

of Charles. The speaker is aware, it is true, of the Roman analogy, and the English state is allowed the benefit of that analogy. But it is well to notice that the speaker does not commit himself to the opinion that the bleeding head is a happy augury:

> And yet in that the *State*
> Foresaw it's happy Fate.

The Roman state was able to take it as a favorable omen, and was justified by the event. With regard to the speaker himself, it seems to me more to the point to notice what prophecy he is willing to commit himself to. He does not prophesy peace. He is willing to predict that England, under Cromwell's leadership, will be powerful in war, and will strike fear into the surrounding states:

> What may not then our *Isle* presume
> While Victory his Crest does plume!
> What may not others fear
> If thus he crown each year!

Specifically, he predicts a smashing victory over the Scots.

But what of the compliments to Cromwell on his ruthlessly effective campaign against the Irish? Does not the speaker succumb, for once, to a bitter and biased patriotism, and does this not constitute a blemish upon the poem?

> And now the *Irish* are asham'd
> To see themselves in one Year tam'd:
> So much one Man can do,
> That does both act and know.

> They can affirm his Praises best,
> And have, though overcome, confest
> How good he is, how just. . . .

Margoliouth glosses the word "confessed" as follows:
"Irish testimony in favor of Cromwell at this moment is highly improbable. Possibly there is a reference to the voluntary submission of part of Munster
with its English colony." But surely Margoliouth in-
dulges in understatement. The most intense partisan
of Cromwell would have had some difficulty in taking
the lines without some inflection of grim irony. The
final appeal in this matter, however, is not to what
Marvell the Englishman must have thought, or even
to what Marvell the author must have intended, but
rather to the full context of the poem itself. In that
context, the lines in question can be read ironically,
and the earlier stanzas sanction that reading. Cromwell's energy, activity, bravery, resolution—even what
may be called his efficiency—are the qualities that have
come in for praise, not his gentleness or his mercy.
The Irish, indeed, are best able to affirm such praise as
has been accorded to Cromwell; and they know from
experience "how good he is, how just," for they have
been blasted by the force of angry Heaven's flame, even
as Charles has been. But I do not mean to turn the passage into sarcasm. The third quality which the speaker
couples with goodness and justice is fitness "for highest
Trust," and the goodness and justice of Cromwell cul-
minate in this fitness. But the recommendation to
trust has reference not to the Irish, but to the English

state. The Irish are quite proper authorities on Cromwell's trustworthiness in this regard, for they have come to know him as the completely dedicated instrument of that state whose devotion to the purpose in hand is unrelenting and unswerving.

To say all this is not to suggest that Marvell shed any unnecessary tears over the plight of the Irish, or even to imply that he was not happy, as one assumes most Englishmen were, to have the Irish rebellion crushed promptly and efficiently. It is to say that the passage fits into the poem—a poem which reveals itself to be no panegyric on Cromwell but an unflinching analysis of the Cromwellian character.

The wild Irish have been tamed, and now the Pict will no longer be able to shelter under his particolored mind. It is the hour of decision, and the particolored mind affords no protection against the man who "does both act and know." In Cromwell's mind there are no conflicts, no teasing mixture of judgments. Cromwell's is not only an "industrious valour," but a "sad valour." Margoliouth glosses "sad" as "steadfast," and no doubt he is right. But sad can mean "sober" also, and I suspect that in this context, with its implied references to Scottish plaids, it means also drab of hue. It is also possible that the poet here glances at one of Virgil's transferred epithets, *maestum timorem,* sad fear, the fear that made the Trojans sad. Cromwell's valor is *sad* in that the Scots will have occasion to rue it.

Thus far the speaker has been content to view Cromwell from a distance, as it were, against the background of recent history. He has referred to him consistently in the third person. But in the last two stanzas, he addresses Cromwell directly. He salutes him as "the Wars and Fortunes Son." It is a great compliment: Cromwell is the son of the wars in that he is the master of battle, and he seems fortune's own son in the success that has constantly waited upon him. But we do not wrench the lines if we take them to say also that Cromwell is the creature of the wars and the product of fortune. The imagery of the early stanzas which treats Cromwell as a natural phenomenon certainly lends support to this reading. Cromwell can claim no sanction for his power in "antient Rights." His power has come out of the wars and the troubled times. I call attention to the fact that we do not have to choose between readings: the readings do not mutually exclude each other: they support each other, and this double interpretation has the whole poem behind it.

Cromwell is urged to march "indefatigably on." The advice is good advice; but it is good advice because any other course of action is positively unthinkable. Indeed, to call it advice at all is perhaps to distort it: though addressed to Cromwell, it partakes of quiet commentary as much as of exhortation. After all, it is restless Cromwell who is being addressed. If he could not cease "in the inglorious Arts of Peace" when his "highest plot" was "to plant the Bergamot," one cannot conceive of his ceasing now in the hour of danger.

> And for the last effect
> Still keep thy Sword erect.

Once more the advice (or commentary) is seriously intended, but it carries with it as much of warning as it does of approval. Those who take up the sword shall perish by the sword: those who have achieved their power on contravention of ancient rights by the sword can only expect to maintain their power by the sword.

What kind of sword is it that is able to "fright the spirits of the shady night"? Margoliouth writes: "The cross hilt of the sword would avert the spirits. . . ." But the speaker makes it quite plain that it is not merely the spirits of the shady night that Cromwell will have to fight as he marches indefatigably on. It will not be enough to hold the sword aloft as a ritual sword, an emblematic sword. The naked steel will still have to be used against bodies less diaphanous than spirits. If there is any doubt as to this last point, Marvell's concluding lines put it as powerfully and explicitly as it can be put:

> The same *Arts* that did *gain*
> A *Pow'r* must it *maintain*.

But, I can imagine someone asking, What is the final attitude toward Cromwell? Is it ultimately one of approval or disapproval? Does admiration overbalance condemnation? Or, is the "Ode," after all, merely a varied Scottish plaid, the reflection of Marvell's own particolored mind—a mind which had not been finally "made up" with regard to Cromwell? I think that enough has been said to make it plain that there is no easy, pat answer to such questions. There is a unified total attitude, it seems to me; but it is so complex that we may oversimplify and distort its complexity by the way in which we put the question. The request for some kind of summing up is a natural one, and I have no wish to try to evade it. For a really full answer, of course, one must refer the questioner to the poem itself; but one can at least try to suggest some aspects of the total attitude.

I would begin by reemphasizing the dramatic character of the poem. It is not a statement—an essay on "Why I cannot support Cromwell" or on "Why I am now ready to support Cromwell." It is a poem essentially dramatic in its presentation, which means that it is diagnostic rather than remedial, and eventuates, not in a course of action, but in contemplation. Perhaps the best way therefore in which to approach it is to conceive of it as, say, one conceives of a Shakespearean tragedy. Cromwell is the usurper who demands and commands admiration. What, for example, is our attitude toward Macbeth? We assume his guilt, but there are qualities which emerge from his guilt which properly excite admiration. I do not mean that the qualities palliate his guilt or that they compensate for his guilt. They actually come into being through his guilt, but they force us to exalt him even as we condemn him. I have chosen an extreme example. I certainly do not mean to imply that in writing the "Ode" Marvell had Shakespeare's tragedy in mind. What I am trying to point to is this: that the kind of honesty and insight and whole-mindedness which we associate with tragedy is to be found to some degree in all great poetry and is to be found in this poem.

R. P. Warren once remarked to me that Marvell has constantly behind him in his poetry the achievement of Elizabethan drama with its treatment of the human will as seen in the perspective of history. He had in mind some of the lyrics, but the remark certainly applies fully to the "Ode." The poet is thoroughly conscious of the drama, and consciously makes use of dramatic perspective. Charles, as we have seen, becomes the "Royal Actor," playing his part on the "Tragick Scaffold." But the tragedy of Charles is merely glanced at. The poem is Cromwell's—Cromwell's tragedy, the first three acts of it, as it were, which is not a tragedy of failure but of success.

Cromwell is the truly kingly man who is *not* king—whose very virtues conduce to kingly power and almost force kingly power upon him. It is not any fumbling on the poet's part which causes him to call Cromwell "a Caesar" before the poem ends, even though he has earlier appropriated that name to Charles. *Both* men are Caesar, Charles the wearer of the purple, and Cromwell, the invincible general, the inveterate campaigner, the man "that does both act and know." Cromwell is the Caesar who must refuse the crown—whose glory it is that he is willing to refuse the crown—but who cannot enjoy the reward and the security that a crown affords. The tension between the speaker's admiration for the kingliness which has won Cromwell the power and his awareness that the power can be maintained only by a continual exertion of these talents for kingship—this tension is never relaxed. Cromwell is not of royal blood—he boasts a higher and a baser pedigree: he is the "Wars and Fortunes Son." He cannot rest because he is restless Cromwell. He must march indefatigably on, for he cannot afford to become fatigued. These implications enrich and qualify an insight into Cromwell which is as heavily freighted with admiration as it is with a great condemnation. But the admiration and the condemnation do not cancel each other. They define each other; and because there is responsible definition, they reinforce each other.

Was this, then, the attitude of Andrew Marvell, born 1621, sometime student at Cambridge, returned traveler and prospective tutor, toward Oliver Cromwell in the summer of 1650? The honest answer must be: I do not know. I have tried to read the poem, the "Horatian Ode," not Andrew Marvell's mind. That seems sensible to me in view of the fact that we have the poem, whereas the attitude held by Marvell at any particular time must be a matter of inference—even though I grant that the poem may be put in as part of the evidence from which we draw inferences. True, we do know that Marvell was capable of composing the "Ode" and I must concede that that fact may tell us a great deal about Marvell's attitude toward Cromwell. I think it probably does. I am not sure, for reasons given earlier in this paper, that it tells us everything: there is the problem of the role of the unconscious in the process of composition, there is the possibility of the poet's having written better than he knew, there is even the matter of the happy accident. I do not mean to overemphasize these matters. I do think, however, that it is wise to maintain the distinction between what total attitude is manifested in the poem and the attitude of the author as citizen.

Yet, though I wish to maintain this distinction, I do not mean to hide behind it. The total attitude realized in the "Ode" does not seem to me monstrously inhuman in its complexity. It could be held by human beings, in my opinion. Something very like it apparently was. Listen, for example, to the Earl of Clarendon's judgment on Cromwell:

He was one of those men, quos vitupare ne inimici quidem possunt, nisi ut simul laudent [whom not even their enemies can inveigh against without at the same time praising them], for he could never have done halfe that mischieve, without great partes of courage and industry and judgement, and he must have had a wonderful understandinge in the nature and humours of men, and as greate a dexterity in the applyinge them, who from a private and obscure birth (though of a good family), without interest of estate, allyance or frenshippes, could rayse himselfe to such a height, and compounde and kneade such opposite and contradictory humours and interests, into a consistence, that contributed to his designes and to ther owne distruction, whilst himselfe grew insensibly powerfull enough, to cutt off those by whom he had climed, in the instant, that they projected to demolish ther owne buildinge. . . .

He was not a man of bloode, and totally declined Machiavells methode . . . it was more then once proposed, that ther might be a generall massacre of all the royall party, as the only expedient to secure the government, but Crumwell would never consent to it, it may be out of to much contempt of his enimyes; In a worde, as he had all the wikednesses against which damnation is denounced and for which Hell fyre is praepared, so he had some virtues, which have caused the memory of some men in all ages to be celebrated, and he will be looked upon by posterity, as a brave, badd man.

The resemblance between Clarendon's judgment and that reflected in the "Ode" is at some points so remarkable that one wonders whether Clarendon had not seen and been impressed by some now lost manuscript of the "Ode": "Who from a private and obscure birth"—"Who, from his private Gardens, where/He liv'd reserved and austere"—"could rayse himself to such a height . . . by whome he had climed"—"Could by industrious Valour climbe," and so on and so forth. But I do not want to press the suggestion of influence of Marvell on Clarendon. Indeed, it makes for my general point to discount the possibility. For what I am anxious to emphasize is that the attitude of the "Ode" is not inhuman in its Olympian detachment, that something like it could be held by a human being, and by a human being of pronounced Royalist sympathies.

I have argued that the critic needs the help of the historian—all the help that he can get—but I have insisted that the poem has to be read as a poem—that what it "says" is a question for the critic to answer, and that no amount of historical evidence as such can finally determine what the poem says. But if we do read the poem successfully, the critic may on occasion be able to make a return on his debt to the historian. If we have read the "Ode" successfully—*if*, I say, for I am far from confident—it may be easier for us to understand how the man capable of writing the

"Ode" was also able to write "Tom May's Death" and "On Appleton House" and indeed, years later, after the Restoration, the statement: "Men ought to have trusted God; they ought and might have trusted the King."

Since completing this essay, I have come upon a further (see p. 144) item which would suggest that the "Horatian Ode" was circulating among Royalists—not Puritans—in the early 1650's. The stanza form of the "Horatian Ode" was used only once by Marvell (in this poem) and does not seem to occur in English poetry prior to Marvell. Margoliouth and Legouis think it probable that this stanza was Marvell's own invention. Perhaps it was. But in Sir Richard Fanshawe's translation of Horace's Odes (*Selected Parts of Horace . . . Now newly put into English,* London, 1652) the "Horatian Ode" stanza is used several times. If Marvell invented the stanza in the summer of 1650, he must have been in close association with Fanshawe for Fanshawe to have borrowed and made use of the stanza so frequently in poems which were to be in print two years later. I suspect that Marvell borrowed the stanza from Fanshawe. Fanshawe had begun to publish translations of Horace (though none in this stanza pattern) as early as 1648 in the volume which contained his translation of *Il Pastor Fido.* But in either case a Royalist connection for Marvell is implied, for Fanshawe (1608–66) was a fervent and active Royalist throughout the war, and after the Restoration was a trusted servant of Charles II.

The following notes appear in H. M. Margoliouth's edition of *The Poems and Letters of Andrew Marvell* (Oxford: Clarendon Press, 1927), I, 237–38:

A correspondent in *The Times Literary Supplement* (29 January 1920) compares with ll. 9–16 of this Ode Lucan, *Pharsalia*, i. 144 *et seq.* . . .

Marvell perhaps had in mind both the Latin (cf. successus urgere suos and "Urg'd his active Star") and Tom May's translation, which here reads as follows (2nd edition, 1631):

But restlesse valour, and in warre a shame
Not to be Conquerour; fierce, not curb'd at all,
Ready to fight, where hope, or anger call,
His forward Sword; confident of successe,
And bold the favour of the gods to presse:
Orethrowing all that his ambition stay,
And loves that ruine should enforce his way;
As lightning by the wind forc'd from a cloude
Breakes through the wounded aire with thunder loud,
Disturbes the Day, the people terrifyes,
And by a light oblique dazels our eyes,
Not *Joves* owne Temple spares it; when no force,
No barre can hinder his prevailing course,
Great waste, as foorth it sallyes and retires,
It makes and gathers his dispersed fires.

Note the verbal resemblances, "restlesse valour" and "industrious Valour," "forward Sword" and "The forward Youth," "lightning . . . from a cloude Breakes" and "Lightning . . . Breaking the Clouds." Further I suggest with diffidence that the striking phrase "active Star" owes something to the chance neighbourhood of the two words in another passage in the same book of May's translation (*Pharsalia,* i. 229–32):

. . . the active Generall
Swifter than Parthian back-shot shaft, or stone
From Balearick Slinger, marches on

T' invade Ariminum; when every star
Fled from th' approaching Sunne but Lucifer . . .

Caesar is up betimes, marching when only the morning star is in the sky: Cromwell urges *his* "active star."

Sir Edward Ridley, carrying on the correspondence in *The Times Literary Supplement* (5 February 1920), points out further a likeness between Marvell's account of the death of Charles I and *Pharsalia,* viii. 613–17 (the death of Pompey):

ut vidit comminus ensem
involvit vultus atque indignatus apertum
fortunae praestare caput, tunc lumina pressit
continuitque animam, ne quas effundere voces
posset et aeternam fletu corrumpere famam . . .

Mr. Dangle's Defense: Acting and Stage History

꽃

By ALAN S. DOWNER

THE FASCINATION of Shakespeare for eighteenth-century critics, and their desire to investigate every aspect of his genius, led to the serious study of stage history. Earlier attempts at recording the history of the stage had been sketchy and rather inaccurate, and had usually some ulterior motive. James Wright's *Historia Histrionica* (1699) is actually another defense of the stage against the onslaughts of Jeremy Collier; John Downes's *Roscius Anglicanus* (1708) is an old prompter's memory book; Colley Cibber (1740) was defending himself, his character, his actions, his tastes. Another old prompter, poor Chetwood, wrote his *History of the Stage* (1749) in a futile attempt to keep out of debtor's prison. His approach is reasonably typical of these early "historians." The first fifteen pages, and they are small ones, of his volume treat of the classical and medieval stage in all countries. In the next seven, he encompasses the Elizabethans. The treatment is about what one might expect:

As the *Stage* flourish'd in the Reign of Queen *Elizabeth* and King *James* the First, with such excellent Dramatic Poets, viz. *Shakespear, Ben Johnson, Massenger,* and many others, we may be well assur'd the *Actors* did not fall much short of the Writers. Nature is the same in every Age. *Taylor, Burbidge, Lowen, Hemmings, Condel, Allen, Mason, Field, Tarlton,* and others that performed in the Plays of *Shakespear, Johnson,* &c. have their public Praises in several cotemporary Authors. Mr. *Marlow,* in his Preface to the *Jew* of *Malta* (a Play acted before King *Charles* the First and his Queen, at *Whitehall,* in the Year 1633) writes, "that Mr. *Mason* and Mr. *Taylor* perform'd their Parts with that Excellence, that it was beyond conceiving."

Given such a passage it is easy to see how Steevens might roundly denounce Chetwood as "a blockhead and a measureless and bungling liar." However, in dealing with the later theater which had come under his own observation, he is nearly always amusing and frequently trustworthy.

Signs of a changing attitude become visible with the first printing of Robert Dodsley's series of Old English Plays in 1744. For this edition, says the publisher, he designed,

by way of Preface, a short historical essay on the rise and progress of the English Stage, from its earliest beginnings, to the death of king Charles the First, when play-houses were suppressed. But in the prosecution . . . I have been so crossed with a want of materials, that I am afraid what I intended should merit thanks, must barely hope for pardon.

If the result, then, is a mere gesture in the direction of stage history, it recognizes, at least, that the background of the times and the conditions of the theater are important for a fuller appreciation of the plays themselves.

Bishop Percy seems to have been the first to attempt an extension of Dodsley. In "The Ballads That Illustrate Shakespeare"—a dissertation attached to Book II of his *Reliques* in 1765—he records such of the notes of his wide reading as apply to the Elizabethan stage. After the inevitable discussion of early dramatic writing, he turns to what he chooses to call the "Œconomy of the English Stage." There is little enough of this, to be sure, drawn mostly from Dodsley and such new sources as Prynne and Flecknoe. There is still nothing on the structure of the theater, or the appointments of the stage. But it was Percy's function —as it was that of the later W. J. Lawrence—to be as much a contributor to other men's researches as to be a historian in his own right. Indeed, in a later edition of the *Reliques,* he takes occasion to point out that Warton in his *History of English Poetry* has inserted "whatever in these volumes fell in with his subject." Warton was only incidentally interested in the theater, of course, but he refers at one point to "those who are professedly making enquiries into the history of our stage from its origin," thus recognizing the distinction which had not hitherto been made clear between the history of the drama and the history of the stage.

"Those who are professedly making enquiries into the history of our stage" were, among others, Steevens,

Ritson, and Malone; and to Edmund Malone surely
belongs (for what it is worth) the title of First Historian of the English Stage. Until the appearance of
Chambers's study in 1923, Malone's *Historical Account of the Rise and Progress of the English Stage,
and of the Economy and Usages of the Ancient
Theatres in England* (1790) was the definitive work
on the subject, not surpassed in accuracy and trustworthiness; limited in its scope only by Malone's consciousness that his time was running out, and by
disagreements with Steevens and "the maniack Ritson."

This history of the stage was but one of several dis-
sertations which Malone intended to affix to a definitive edition of Shakespeare's works, an edition which
Walpole was to characterize as "the heaviest of all
books . . . with notes that are an extract of all the
opium that is spread through the works of all the bad
playwrights of that age." Malone had to some extent
anticipated this sort of criticism: he wrote Bishop
Percy that "Shakespeare is a stout horse and will carry
a great weight. I hope we shall not break his back at
last." Some idea of his indefatigability in seeking out
information will be gained from a glance at his sources.
He uses old plays, Hentzner, the *Historia Histrionica,*
Herbert's office books, Prynne, the Lord Chamber-
lain's Manuscripts, Inner Temple Manuscripts, Cam-
den, Stowe, Heywood's *Apology,* Winwood's *Memorials,* Flecknoe, Gosson, *The Gull's Hornbook,* White-
lock's *Memorials,* newspapers, Downes and Aubrey,
among others. His principal object is "as accurate a

delineation of the internal form and economy of our ancient theatres, as the distance at which we stand, and the obscurity of the subject will permit." For the first time, some attempt is made to reconstruct the Elizabethan theater as different from the theater of the eighteenth century. Confining himself largely to the Globe and Blackfriars because these were Shakespeare's theaters, Malone reproduces an exterior cut of the former from the Antwerp view of London, recognizes the existence of an upper stage and the circular nature of the auditorium. He does not understand the inner stage, or concomitantly the use of front curtains. He collects information on stage music, properties, lighting, discusses whether it was customary to ride on horseback to the play (because Shakespeare was a horseholder), and includes some information on copyright and payment of authors, and catcalling. For the first time, also, Malone assembles information about the actors of the early theater—limiting himself of course to those named in the First Folio, and paying particular attention to clowns, since this will be a specific illustration for *Hamlet*.

But a scholar's work, and Malone's in particular, is never done. While the *Essay* was in press, the great mass of Alleyn Manuscripts at Dulwich College came to light, and was "transmitted" to Malone. He is thus enabled to append a sort of transcript of Henslowe's *Diary,* confining himself to playlists, receipts, and inventories.

This matter of the Alleyn papers being "transmitted" to Malone is one to make the contemporary stage historian turn green. But it was by no means unique in Malone's experience. As he is writing, he informs the reader, Herbert's office book "is now before me." And on September 21, 1793, he writes to Percy:

at Stratford I spent ten days, by permission of the Corporation, in rummaging all their stores. I am confident I unfolded and slightly examined not less than three thousand papers and parchments; several of which were as old as the time of Henry the Fourth, and probably had not been opened for two centuries. From the whole mass I selected whatever I thought likely to throw any light upon the Life of Shakespeare, on which I am now employed; and these the Mayor very obligingly permitted me to pack up in a box and bring with me to London, that I might peruse them at my leisure.

Malone's successors have followed two lines, further research into the economy of the Elizabethan theater, and more general studies of both the Elizabethan and the later stage. The Economists, the searchers after details, were headed by such as Halliwell-Phillips, and other contributors to the Shakespeare Society and *Notes and Queries*—Shakespeare is still their cloak of respectability—and culminating in the work of W. J. Lawrence. The more general historians include such various scholars as Genest, Collier, Summers, and Nicoll.

The chief end of recent antiquaries has been the more or less final determination of the structure, appearance, and facilities of the Elizabethan public theater. With the exception of certain minor, but I venture to think important, details the various playing areas and their relationships have been agreed upon. In John C. Adams's *Globe Playhouse,* the student has now available for him a thoroughly practicable realization of the physical structure for which the Elizabethan playwright adapted his work. Mr. Adams further suggests the methods of staging, the uses to which the areas were put. Professor G. F. Reynolds, concerning himself with the Red Bull, mainly from a consideration of texts is able to recreate another and perhaps older form of staging, the use of simultaneous settings on the formal stage, while the researches of Lawrence on the Fortune, and Wallace on Blackfriars suggest the common conventions and the individual divergences of the various playhouses.

As a result, it is now possible to visualize an Elizabethan play *in production,* and to realize how much of his technique for a man like Shakespeare was governed by the theater for which he wrote, and what effects were possible to him because of it. The nineteenth-century traditions of Shakespearean production had largely destroyed any feeling for the form of his plays. Frequent changes of complex realistic settings had led either to unconscionable stage waits or to ruthless cutting and transposition of scenes. This may have something to do with the overwhelming interest in character development which is so prominent a feature of both ninteenth-century acting and nineteenth-century criticism. But once the investigators had probed the secret of Elizabethan stage architecture, and William Poel had experimented with the plays on a copy of the Elizabethan stage, new light was thrown upon the playwright's practice and purpose.

This might be illustrated by quoting almost any one of Granville-Barker's wise *Prefaces to Shakespeare,* or Miss Ellis-Fermor's recent and highly successful analysis of *Troilus and Cressida.* For the sake of brevity, however, I have chosen to speak of one scene in *The Winter's Tale* which is considerably illuminated by some knowledge of the theatrical conventions for which it was written. The Elizabethan audience had long been accustomed to the prologue before the play, especially the simple prologue of *Fulgens and Lucrece* (1497):

> Peace, no more words, for now they come,
> The players been even here at hand,

or of *Dr. Faustus* (*c.*1589), perhaps with the drawing of the traverse curtain:

> And this the man that in his study sits.
> *Enter Faustus in his study.*

There was also a more complex type of prologue, one which was digested into the play, as in *The Old Wives' Tale* of 1590. You will remember that in this play we first meet three delightful fellows who have lost their way in the woods. Taken in hand by the local smith, they are fed and put up for the night. To pass the time, the old wife Madge begins to spin a yarn.

Once upon a time [she says], there was a king, or a lord, or a duke, that had a fair daughter, the fairest that ever was; as white as snow and as red as blood: and once upon a time his daughter was stolen away: and he sent all his men to seek out his daughter; and he sent so long, that he sent all his men out of his land. . . . O Lord, I quite forgot! there was a conjurer, and this conjurer could do anything, and he turned himself into a great dragon, and carried the king's daughter away in his mouth to a castle that he made of stone; and there he kept her I know not how long, till at last all the king's men went out so long that her two brothers went to seek her. O, I forget! she (he, I would say) turned a proper young man to a bear at night, and a man in the day, and keeps by a cross that parts three several ways; and he made his lady run mad,—Ods me bones, who comes here?

And enter the Two Brothers to tell gammer's tale for her, with action, and in just such rambling fashion as she has begun. To maintain the perspective the prologue characters remain on the stage throughout, and Madge occasionally interrupts with a comment to remind us that this is her story.

It has long been a commonplace of criticism that *The Winter's Tale* falls into two parts and is thus defective structurally. It is certainly dangerous, to say the least, to attack Shakespeare's structure any more, or to pretend that *Othello* is better than *Hamlet* because it is more like a well-made play. An examination of *The Winter's Tale* will show that it falls into three parts, not two, and that it is more carefully integrated than has been heretofore acknowledged. The major break is of course the speech of Time at the beginning of the Fourth Act. But there is an earlier one in Act II, Scene i. Let us try to visualize it, on that vast projecting platform of the public theater. Hermione enters through one of the doors at the back or side of the stage with her ladies whom she orders to take the boy to them, referring to Mamillius who troubles her past endur-

ing. "Come, my gracious lord," says the First Lady
and the group draws away from the Queen to indulge
in a dozen lines of precocious banter. During these
speeches they move towards the front of the stage
where they will be more visible and more audible,
keeping always apart from the Queen who does not
hear their comments on her pregnancy. "What wisdom
stirs among you?" she asks, and, her spirits returned,
summons the boy to her to entertain her with a story.
He begins, she interrupts, "Nay, come sit down; then
on." How careful Shakespeare is to place these characters in an exact position, so grouped that when Mamillius resumes he whispers the tale in the Queen's ear
and, I feel certain, at the front of the stage, since
Leontes is allowed over twenty lines to come up with
them. The entrance of Leontes for the audience will
have a certain ambivalence: he enters as the revenging
cuckold *and* as the man who dwelt by the churchyard
in the tale of sprites and goblins. Hermione's reaction
suits with this ambivalence. "What is this? sport?" she
asks. On one level then the rest of *The Winter's Tale*
is a comedy in which Time makes and unfolds error,
ending with the triumph of young love and old. On
the other level there is Mamillius, who does not waken
like Madge at the end of his tale. Mamillius is dead,
and Shakespeare mentions him in the last act just often
enough to lend a bitterness to the sweetness of his conclusion. "A sad tale's best for winter."

The other line of post-Malone investigation, the
general history of the stage, is marked not only by the

utilization of the specialist's researches into economy to make new surveys of the Elizabethan theater, but by a broadening of interests to include the stage history of later periods. Of the first of these, the synthesizers, the most prominent figures are probably Collier, Fleay, and Chambers, though each was also an investigator on his own, and Collier was a creative artist and perhaps something more. The work of Sir Edmund Chambers is so widely known that it need only be pointed out as the culmination of Elizabethan stage scholarship. He began, like all the rest, with the intention of writing a life of Shakespeare, for which he felt certain preliminary investigations were necessary. At the end of two volumes on the Medieval stage and four on the Elizabethan, he began to wonder whether the biography would ever be started, let alone finished. These six volumes are encyclopedic in their comprehensiveness, covering every aspect of the theater and the drama except acting—an omission which several investigators have attempted to remedy with partial success. Incidentally, though Chambers stops with the Elizabethan theater, Professor G. E. Bentley is carrying on the work for the theater under James and Charles with equal inclusiveness.

Studies of the later theater may be said to begin with the biographies of James Boaden, the early nineteenth-century hack. In a rambling, almost dateless fashion (quite, I am afraid, in the theatrical tradition), he sets down the memoirs of J. P. Kemble, Mrs. Siddons, and Dorothy Jordan, the whole intended as a history of the stage during his own time. In strong contrast is John

Genest's modestly titled *Some Account of the English Stage,* published in ten large volumes in 1832, and utterly dependent upon dates. Genest, a clergyman whose ill-health forced his retirement to Bath, during ten years of great suffering before his death put together in chronological order a series of annotated playbills from the Restoration to his own day. He most considerately sums up the plots of plays too dismal to read, provides casts, lives of actors, criticisms, accounts of theatrical matters: all in a kind of shorthand, and for the most part in the bad temper which so often accompanies ill-health. For all its tricksiness it is the first complete and trustworthy outline of the eighteenth-century theater, still a dependable guide and mine of information. Genest's method, if we may judge from his scrapbooks, was to clip the theater advertisements from the daily papers, together with such gossip and information as appeared with them, and summarize. Whether more time and better health might have produced a more graceful and unified whole it is impossible to say. A revision, or redoing, of Genest's work is now under way, but it will be many years in coming; there was, we have discovered, a good deal that never got into the papers.

The Restoration drama and stage has been the special province of the Reverend Montague Summers who has collected as widely apparently as W. J. Lawrence, and finds himself (like Malone) surrounded by maniack Ritsons. His published volumes are as difficult to use as a scholarly work may well be and, though his intention was to do for the Restoration what Chambers did for the Elizabethan theater, there seems little hope for either an orderly picture or the completion of the task. Allardyce Nicoll will probably continue to be the primary resort of future investigators, at least until the new Genest is available. Nicoll's wide knowledge of the theater and his untiring researches have produced a mighty shelf—including the most basic of tools, the volumes on the English stage from the Restoration to 1900. It may seem ungrateful to refer to them as tools, but surely their chief value lies rather in their handlists of plays than in their texts, which are limited in scope. The incompleteness of the handlists is frequently noted together with a sufficient number of inaccuracies but, and this is particularly true for the nineteenth century, Nicoll was working new territory and had set himself a good deal of ground to cover. It is not surprising if a few nuggets got overlooked or misplaced.

Research in the post-Restoration theater has just begun and much remains to do. Not I think so much in chronology; that is reasonably well established. What we need is full investigation of the details of production, costuming, lighting, scenery, and so forth. We need to reconstruct the stages and the productions as has been done for the Globe. George C. D. Odell has shown the way in his survey of the history of Shakespearean production from Betterton to Irving. But this is only a start: we need to find promptbooks and analyze them, we need to find sketches and stage plans. The account books in the Folger Library, for example, should be examined for the production details they reveal: Dr. Giles Dawson has discovered that Cibber regularly entered the expense of a bushel of mold for the graveyard scene in *Hamlet*, a surprising evidence of realism in early eighteenth-century staging, and there must be many more.

As for the American theater, nearly everything is to do. Local histories are badly needed; no over-all picture can be drawn until they are reasonably complete, since until recent years the American theater was not a metropolitan theater as in England. It was a theater on rivers and in mining camps, in boats, under canvas, on the stages of a thousand opera houses. It was not two competing repertory companies but a nationwide chain of stock companies, of touring combinations, of visiting stars. All this must be thoroughly investigated: not as thoroughly I suppose as Odell's monumental history of the New York stage, but in such fashion (to mention only two of a gradually growing list of local histories) Schoberlin's *From Candles to Footlights* and MacMinn's *Theatre of the Golden Era in California.* Here we have uncovered the wondrous stories of John S. Langrishe and Caroline Chapman and Lola Montes. But where is the story of Alexander Drake, of Sol Smith, of the Chapman's showboat, of Nugent and Gleason's Metropolitans, of the Nigger Minstrel?

Perhaps the most complex aspect of stage history is the study of actors and acting. It is sufficiently remote from the history of literature. Your own experience will tell you that in the contemporary theater, the actor as the more immediate artist (and much to the despair of the playwright) is usually credited with the wit or the emotion or the insight which has been created for him. Your reading will tell you that dead actors are little more than pegs to hang good anecdotes on. On the one hand then, the actor is sneered at by literary critics as a mere tool of the author, like his pen, no artist at all, and on the other he becomes a glamorous personality building sand castles on the seacoast of Bohemia. Yet the tritest of stage aphorisms declares the actor to be the abstract and brief chronicle of his time, and unlike a good many stage aphorisms, this seems capable of proof.

It will be well first to consider this matter of glamor and Bohemianism on which theatrical writers are so insistent. It is certainly the primary appeal of the stage —the atmosphere of unreality or fairyland which is so attractive to the adolescent and which carries over into adulthood as the fairyland of unconventionality, if not downright immorality. The historical novel gets on the best-seller lists not for its interpretation of history but for its depiction of an age free from the restraints and repressions which apparently all novel readers sense in their own lives. So with stage biography. The recent life of the late John Barrymore is a case in point: a monstrous picture of a dipsomaniac Don Juan and his reckless *descensus Averni,* with hardly a suggestion that Barrymore was if only for a moment a great actor, that he had been (as the ablest of the English critics pointed out recently) the finest Hamlet of the post-Irving period.

This tendency to think of actors as characters in a

drama, as the fictitious beings they portray, is the first obstacle that the stage historian must surmount. He will be only incidentally concerned with testing the scandalous rumors of the parentage of Sir William Davenant, with enumerating the extramarital adventures of Mme. Vestris, or the unprintable exuberances of Edwin Forrest. We have learned to subordinate such matters in studying the accomplishments of Marlowe and Boswell and Byron and even Wilde, though it has been something of a struggle. If we are to be serious stage historians we must learn what belongs to history and what to the smoking room.

It is not easy. If today all that is written about a Hollywood star is a record of trips to Reno, or drunken brawls in night clubs, the same was largely true in the past. Few indeed are the great actors or great actresses who have not furnished the principal figure in a scandalous chronicle. About half of what we know about Burbage consists of an amorous anecdote, and he is only the beginning. The egoisms of Colley Cibber, the sarcasms of Quin, the drunkenness of Kean, these are all writ large on the record. Like Barrymore, as artists they scarcely exist. The student of the history of acting must discover the artist beneath the cloak of glamor and make plain the meaning of his achievement.

Without passing judgment on current stage scholarship, I want to select and comment on three books which seem to me models for the stage historian and the student of acting in particular. I cannot report on their reception by the public; I would suppose that none of the three challenged the best-seller position of Mr. Fowler's *Good Night, Sweet Prince* (the unwitting irony of that title is equaled only by the vulgarity of the choice) or Miss Armstrong's *Fanny Kemble, Passionate Victorian*. But the stage historian must reconcile himself to the fact that the public no more wants to know the truth of the actor's mystery than of the poet's or the musician's.

The first of these books in order of appearance is H. N. Hillebrand's *Life of Edmund Kean*. Now Kean is the worst of traps for the historian: his life was a succession of Bohemian incidents from a birth shrouded in mystery to a death soaked in alcohol. Three previous biographers could only stand agape before the record of divorce, debauchery, and riot. Without attempting to gloss over the private life of his subject, however, Professor Hillebrand set about illustrating Coleridge's famous definition of Kean's method, examining the records of his performances in detail, and producing a model biography.

Like Kean, Edwin Forrest is a trap for the unwary, since he was involved not only in divorce and riot, but in politics. The recent study by Montrose Moses—which had even more stubborn official and partisan biographies to contend with—is not, like Professor Hillebrand's, an analysis of an actor's achievement. It is rather a picture of Forrest as the crystallization of the spirit of his time. The Astor Place Riot, which was inspired if not sponsored by Forrest, is clearly seen as an aspect of the ring-tailed-roarer period of America's youth, and Forrest emerges as the stage counterpart of

Colonel Sellers, or a character from *Martin Chuzzle-wit*. Mr. Moses' volume is a useful model of the study of an actor as the manifestation of his era.

Of the third volume, a work of pure scholarship, I should like to speak more at length. This is Arthur Colby Sprague's *Shakespeare and the Actors*. Professor Sprague, after a seven-year search through prompt-books, memoirs, and a depressing tonnage of old newspaper files, has recorded in a fascinating study all the significant stage business employed by Shakespearean actors from the Restoration to the death of Irving. He has traced the history—origin, development, and (sometimes) disuse—of such familiar pieces of textual illumination as the gravedigger's waistcoats, the concluding embrace in the nunnery scene, the smothering of Desdemona. He notes such pieces of sheer foolishness as Fechter's mirror in *Othello*, Barry Sullivan's prosy teasing of Polonius, and the shrieking, the sliding, and the tumbler's tricks indulged in by such celebrated nineteenth-century Juliets as Miss Jarman, Fanny Kemble, and Stella Colas. But the reader must search diligently to find, amidst a great mass of faithfully recorded detail, such evidences of the stupidity of actors. The conclusion is inescapable that a good actor at work is not unintelligent and that the anonymous critic was not far wrong in declaring the good player to be the best commentator.

Perhaps this is not very startling. The actor after all is working within a frame of conventions which he has inherited from his predecessors. And stage history, if it shows anything at all, certainly makes it plain that the conventions of the stage are not superimposed rules but practical devices which have been developed over the centuries to enable the playwright and the actor to convey ideas to an audience. This is a point worth making, for the tendency of Shakespearean critics in the last century has been to get farther and farther from the stage. Indeed many of the more astute and most widely followed of the modern commentators (to say nothing of the Romantic critics and Professor Bradley) seem to have forgotten as they turn the pages of *Hamlet* or *Lear* in their studies that they are dealing with plays at all, plays which are bounded by the physical limitations of a particular theater, and the conventions acceptable to the actors and audience of a particular time. When actors err, as Professor Sprague indicates, it is often because they are being super-subtle, attempting to transcend (or ignore), as the closet critic often does, these physical limitations. Fechter directed his Horatio at the line, "I'll cross it, though it blast me," to *cross himself;* Mrs. Siddons made a face "as if she perceived a *foul* smell," when washing her hands as Lady Macbeth; the Imogen of Helen Faucit called at the mouth of the cave in the forest and ran from the sound she herself had made. More famous is the business at the end of II, vi, of *The Merchant of Venice.* Traditionally, the scene had ended with the elopement of Jessica and Lorenzo. In Irving's production, Shylock reentered and the curtain fell as he rapped expectantly on the door of his empty house. Developing this idea, Mansfield's Shylock ransacked the house and rushed out yelling, while a Christian crowd hooted; Nat Goodwin emerged wailing, bearing a letter which Jessica had found time to write him; Benson, Daly, Otis Skinner, George Arliss—all have had their variations of this interpretive business. Unfortunately in such a scene the business seems planned to interpret the player rather than the playwright.

But when such pieces of added pantomime and over-subtle, overliteral gesture are wrong in the terms of the contemporary theater, audiences and critics do not hesitate to set the actor right. The actor's errors are quickly determined at the box office. For the actor has a special task—he is not merely as the scholar and literary critic the interpreter of the text of Shakespeare, he *is* the play to his immediate audience. And it is his unique problem to illuminate in a passing moment what the author has set down. There is no time in the theater, and there should be no necessity, for going back over the chain of reasoning which lies behind an interpretation: the actor is either immediately right, or forever wrong. It is surely no longer necessary to plead that Shakespeare's plays were not written to be mulled over in the study. Their inconsistencies of plotting and characterisation can be reasoned away by dint of much throwing about of brains, but in the hands of a capable cast, as the author intended, the inconsistencies are not apparent. The argumentative pleasure of the scholar and critic disputing over Hamlet's madness in the public print is a secondary or derivative pleasure; the primary pleasure of *Hamlet* is to experience it in the public theater.

Let me quote the highest authority I know on this point. "I say," wrote Harley Granville-Barker,

that the scholar and actor have need of each other. And here is my main contention. Dramatic art does demand the service of pure scholarship—and in the case of a period such as the Elizabethan, so uncertainly documented, and with the threads of its tradition so broken— of various sorts of scholarship. But drama can only be profitably considered in its full integrity. We may have, for the purposes of its service, to treat separately of its literary, its technical, its histrionic aspects. But unless, while doing so, we can still visualize the plays as completed things—living in the theater—we shall always tend to be astray in our conclusions about them.

The actor, then, can frequently illuminate the text as a critic lacking the knowledge of the technical resources and limitations of the stage must fail to do. But perhaps of wider interest is the light which the actor, quite unconsciously, throws upon his audience. This is not always true of the great writers who may represent a specialized interest, a minor trend, or a taste which the future will develop. The actor cannot wait for his fame—which explains, I think, why the actor is so often open to the reproach of choosing a bad play as a vehicle in preference to what a later age will recognize as an infinitely better one. It will also help to explain, I think, why actors will turn to Shakespeare or Ibsen or Shaw, secure in the knowledge that they are employing their talents on a recognized work of art, and that their reputation will not suffer by being associated with *Cato, Pizzaro, The Bells,* or *The Green Goddess.* An analysis of at least the last three of these plays would to some extent provide an index to the taste of their times, but it would be a weariness to the soul to undertake it. It is no weariness to study Shakespeare, and to study what an actor does in Shakespeare is doubly fascinating, particularly if he is a popularly successful actor.

To illustrate this last point, and in conclusion, I would like to summarize a famous performance of *Macbeth.* The actor and producer was William Charles Macready, and Macbeth was his favorite role, the one in which he took his farewell of the stage, the one which his critics were most nearly unanimous in selecting as his great Shakespearean part. He performed it first in 1820 and his farewell benefit fell in 1851. Between those dates he gave several hundred performances of the part and since he was a scholarly and conscientious man, the performances were rarely exactly alike; he was continually *making experiments,* adding and subtracting pieces of business which he felt would make clearer to his audience the underlying meaning of the character and the play. For Macready's purpose, said *The Spectator,* was to *familiarize* the creations of the dramatist to the audience, to bring them into focus with the auditor's own understanding of humanity and natural law.

The production was based upon the contrast and juxtaposition of three themes.[1] The stage lamps are

[1] The description which follows is a pastiche made up of contemporary reviews and items from the original promptbook in the Princeton Library. I have kept the original wording wherever possible and abstained from using quotation marks to give as nearly as can be the effect of the performance. For a fuller and documented descrip-

dimmed as the curtain rises to the sound of rain and
thunder. Lightning sweeps across the background. In
the center of the darkened stage stand the three weird
sisters, heads together, three horrible figures whose
beards and short kirtles give them a definitely masculine appearance. After a moment, they separate, moving apart until the first witch halts them with the opening lines of the play. At the end they disappear, having
established the first theme, the tremendous evil which
hangs over the play—three supernatural beings met
for a moment, and going at once about their works of
darkness.

The next scene establishes the second theme, the
power and glory of majesty, with the first of a series of
processional entrances: two chamberlains, Duncan,
Malcolm and Donalbain, a physician, Lenox, three
officers and six lords. Each entrance of Duncan in the
play is preceded by a procession, each procession
grander than the last, culminating in the reception at
Macbeth's castle (I, iv). First come a seneschal and
four officers, next two chamberlains with torches, Duncan, Malcolm, Donalbain; Macduff, Banquo, and
Fleance in a group; Lenox, Rosse, and the ubiquitous
physician in a group; and six lords (gentlemen of the
ballet) to fill up the gaps. A counter procession begins
to arrive on the scene from the castle during Banquo's
description of the establishment. This is led by four
servants with torches, followed by six ladies, Lady
Macbeth, and Seyton with a torch—a crowded scene,

tion, see "Macready's Production of *Macbeth*," *Quarterly Journal of
Speech,* April, 1947.

made colorful and glittering by the torchlight. To this
is added a Royal March from off stage as Duncan begs
to be conducted to his host, and the doubled procession moves with dignity into the castle: seneschal, four
officers, two chamberlains, Duncan and Lady Macbeth,
six ladies, Malcolm and Donalbain, Macduff, Banquo
and Fleance, the physician, six lords and four servants.
This is not meaningless show, but establishes the background of majesty against which the terrible story takes
place.

The third theme, which is most characteristic of
Macready, begins with the letter scene. Macbeth enters
and embraces his wife, a traditional piece of business
for which there is little warrant in the text. She greets
him, but through her speech his restlessness is apparent, his lips moving involuntarily until at last the
words burst from him, "My dearest love, Duncan comes
here tonight." In reply to his Lady's "And when goes
hence?" he says quickly, "Tomorrow," as if merely
stating a fact, pausing for a second, looking at her, and
then continuing in a lower tone and a slow and conscious manner, "—as he purposes." The seventh scene,
an anteroom of the castle, continues the establishment of this theme. A lamp is burning in the room,
and at the back of the stage is an entrance beyond
which, occasionally, servants pass bearing torches and
dishes of food, a thoroughly realistic and domestic interpretation of the original stage direction. All this is
to establish the third theme, the human and recog-
nizable relationship between a man and his wife in

their home, a theme from which Macready will extract the last ounce of pathos.

The opening scenes of the second act are played in the courtyard of Macbeth's castle, an enormous walled square filling the entire stage. The first part of the scene is played in darkness, lighted by the torches of Banquo's servant and Seyton. At their exit, Macbeth is alone, silent, like a man on the verge of fate, when suddenly, raising his hand, he sees the dagger wavering about in the air. He does not start at it. Rather he keeps his eye constantly on the painting of his fear, recoiling and advancing to the dread object of his struggling excitement. As he comes to the end, the bell strikes twice off stage; in an almost imploring voice he cries,

> Hea-hear it not, Duncan, for it is a knell
> That summons thee to heaven or to hell,

pointing upward and downward. He disappears into the King's chamber, with a crouching form and a stealthy felonlike step, pausing when part way through the door so that his left leg and foot remain tremblingly in sight for a moment.

The sounds of rain and thunder roll forth loud and long as Lady Macbeth comes on stage, the thunder punctuating her speech and thoroughly muffling Macbeth's off-stage cry and her response. Suddenly Macbeth rushes on stage, two daggers clicking like castanets in his hand. His face is white; hands and daggers are stained with gore. In a broken and terrifying whisper he says, "I have done the deed. Didst thou not hear a noise?" He infuses additional pathos into his need of blessing by repetition: "Amen stuck—stuck in my throat." Lady Macbeth finishes the crime, the knocking commences, and Macbeth's lamentations for his lost innocence become fearfully bitter. As the Lady returns, he buries his face in his arms, and the knocking continues until his agonizing howl: "Wake Duncan with thy knocking. I would *thou* COULDST!" He stands with his face turned from his wife and his arms outstretched to the irrecoverable past. As she drags him from the stage to their chambers, nothing remains but darkness and the sound of knocking.

The domestic theme is further amplified by III, ii, which Macready fills full of pathos and remorse. "Duncan is in his grave. After life's fitful fever *he* sleeps well," is spoken in tones of hopeless yearning, and a heavy sigh trembles through the theater. And, as Lady Macbeth questions him as to what is to be done with Banquo and Fleance, he turns from her with a furtive look—the guilty man is alone, isolated even from the partner of his crime. He gives a sinister, ill-suppressed laugh: "Be innocent of the knowledge, dearest chuck. . . ."

The theme of majesty is turned to ironic use in the banquet scene. The opening is truly spectacular. In the center of the great hall is a raised dais with two throne-chairs, one on the right for the Queen, one on the left for Macbeth. A page stands beside each, and below them, Seyton and the physician (who seems to go with the crown). Directly before the dais on the floor is placed a table with two chairs at either end; two more long tables on either side extend from mid-stage almost to the footlights, with the guests seated about them. At the back, on either side, are grouped soldiers. The tables are piled high with most splendid fruits, and gorgeous dish covers glitter in endless perspective. Servants, gathered at the center table, move to right and left to serve the banqueters, and music adds to the high festivity of the beginning.

Contrast this with the ending: Macbeth, collapsed in the chair lately left by Banquo's ghost, the guests departed in confusion, and Lady Macbeth sunk in despair at the end of one of the tables. All this is preparation for what is to come, Lady Macbeth's death, the desertion of the thanes, and Macbeth's desperate resolution to pursue the course which his crime has set him upon.

The three themes, of evil, majesty, and domesticity, are brought together in the final movement of the production which begins in V, iii. Macbeth enters with a proud expression of haughty self-complacency, his head thrown back, his lip curling with scorn, as he asks, "What's the *boy*, Malcolm?" A moment later, after the cream-faced loon has brought his information, Macbeth sinks into deep and melancholy pathos, "I have lived long enough . . ." his whole body relaxing, as nerveless as his mind. The mood passes, as Seyton brings him news that arouses his determination. "Give me mine armor!" he thunders imperiously, then seeing the physician suddenly alters his voice and manner to ask colloquially, "How does your patient, Doc-

tor?" The contrast is extreme, but is intended to remind us that beneath the martial exterior there is a
simple and loving husband, distraught about his wife.
After the physician has made his reply, Macbeth strides
back to Seyton to have his armor buckled on, turning
in intervals of stormy chiding to direct inquiries or
splenetic remarks, and at the last rushing off to meet
the approaching foe.

In his next scene, Macbeth enters with Seyton and
some of his soldiers, throwing his brag at the enemy.
He has wound up his courage to the very highest pitch
once more, only to be shaken, first by the cry of women
within, then by Seyton's report of the Queen's death.
His baton falls from his hand, hinting at his grief, and
suggesting that his hold on his position is perilously un-
certain. For a moment, he stands silent, the very mus-
cles of his face slackened, and then begins, "She should
have died hereafter; There would have been a time
for such a word." A pause, then, "To—morrow,—and
tomorrow,—and tomorrow," slowly and haltingly at
first, conveying the agony of his mind; then as if struck
by the thought which follows, he goes rapidly through
the famous passage. There is no excitement in his
reading, only a withering calm, a controlled agony. His
voice is chill with despair, his look blank and desolate.

In the next scene, the English army marches on
stage, each man completely screened by the immense
bough he carries. At Malcolm's command, "Your leavy
screens thrown down," the real soldiers at the front
obey, and at the same time those painted on the back-

drop as stretching away in the distance seem to do the same, with the assistance of the stage carpenters.

All, however, is but preparation for the climactic moment of the play: the death duel between Macduff and Macbeth. The scene is on the ramparts of the castle, with a great iron gate in the background. Macbeth enters, determined not to commit suicide. At that, the gates are burst open with a tremendous shout and Macduff rushes on crying, "Turn hellhound, turn!" Macbeth warns him off, but Macduff engages him with his sword. After a few passes, Macbeth throws him back, his countenance flushed with conscious security, with an expression of ineffable contempt. Holding his sword with careless ease, he announces that he bears a charmed life. Macduff counters with the story of his nativity, and the effect on Macbeth is wondrous. Like a man about to be devoured by a wild beast, he stands gazing on his enemy in breathless horror as if all the sinews of his frame had relaxed in one moment. "I'll not fight with thee!" he cries, and retreats toward the castle.

Macduff's taunts of "coward" and "show and gaze o'th'time," awaken in him his martial ardor. He turns upon his fate, and stands at bay. His eye kindles, his bosom swells, his head is upreared in defiance, and, deserted by fate and metaphysical aid, he summons up his honest power to fight and die like a hero. The swordsmen rush upon each other and after a few desperate passes, Macbeth receives his death wound and staggers back. He catches himself, and with a momen-

tary suggestion of his regal stride returns, only to fall
upon Macduff's sword in yielding weakness. The
spirit fights, but the body sinks in mortal faintness.
Thrusting his sword into the ground, he raises himself
by its help to his knees where he stares full in the face
of his vanquisher with a resolute and defiant gaze of
concentrated Majesty, Hate, and Knowledge, and falls
dead, as Malcolm and the thanes enter. To the general
cry of "Hail, King of Scotland," the curtain falls.

Such in part was the performance. It becomes even
more interesting if you trace the additional business
that was experimented with. At one time, in III, ii,
Macready tried a novel manifestation of tenderness
toward his wretched wife. To a critic of 1836, this
seemed vastly misplaced and wrong. To a critic of 1850
it was a further insight into the mind of Macbeth. In
1849, during one of the King's ravings at the ghost of
Banquo, the physician stepped forward and gave Lady
Macbeth—in pantomime—a medical opinion of her
husband's sanity. In 1849 this was wrong. But in 1870?

From the over-all picture of Macready's *Macbeth*
what emerges? Nothing so simple, I fear, as the Shakespearean hero turned eminent Victorian. Rather, it is a
subtle mirror of the state of mind which was harden-
ing into Victorianism. There is the illustration of the
text in the handling of the witches, the processions
which accompany Duncan, the mechanical devices
which make plain the tricks of the English army. There
is the increasing realism of banquets and battles, and
setting, and costumes. There is the development of

domestic interest: for as a minor critic of the day declared, "A subject to come home to the hearts and bosoms of men must be of a domestic nature." Macready did to Macbeth and Lear and the rest what Tennyson did to the Knights of the Table Round. And there is clear emphasis upon the moral of the play. To Westland Marston, the whole piece hung upon the contrast between Macready's first entrance as the free-walking, upright warrior, and his felonlike creeping into the King's bedchamber.

And not the least, of course, the amplification of the excitements of the play, particularly the final duel with Macduff, which is a part of the love of violence reflected in the general acting of the time, in the attraction of melodrama, of crime fiction, of hairbreadth rescues, of slashing journalism, and so on. For an audience not yet ready for the elegancies of Tom Robertson, the repressed force of Alfred Wigan and, say, Forbes-Robertson, Macready's Macbeth was typical entertainment.

Stage history is thus a legitimate field for literary research. It must frequently deal, to be sure, with paint and lathe and box-office receipts, and with personalities that are rather remote from the written word. But the purpose of the theater is to interpret a special kind of written words. By coming at a knowledge of the theatrical conventions of the time we may come at a surer estimate of a playwright's work. And from the actors and the audiences of the past we may learn much which will illuminate cultural history. Perhaps this whole essay might be taken as a sort of defense of the Mr. Dangle who, as Sheridan thought, foolishly said, "I say the stage is the Mirror of Nature and the actors are the Abstract and Brief Chronicles of the time: and pray what can a man of sense study better?"

The Textual Approach
to Meaning

※

By E. L. McADAM, JR.

THE TEXTUAL CRITIC is an optimistic and plodding soul who hopes someday to produce an edition of an author much superior to any which that author himself ever saw through the press. Unlikely as this sounds, it is not impossible, since such a scholar is a specialist in the pitfalls which lie in the path between the author's words, as yet perhaps not committed to ink, and the printed book at the end.

The textual critic is primarily concerned with finding out what his author said. It may seem that this is the case of every type of scholar, but it is particularly the purpose of the textual critic. Like most other critics, he is interested in what the author meant, but being a dull sort, he first wishes to be assured of the very words. These are frequently distorted in the most unsuspected ways. To start at a beginning, the author, in dictating, may mislead by a provincial pronunciation, and sometimes a careless secretary will write down a word of similar sound. For example, in the *Christabel* manuscript designated *W* by E. H. Coleridge in the Oxford edition of Coleridge's *Poems,* we find some typical mistakes by Mary Hutchinson of similar words (the first is the correct reading)—sinful: simple (l. 353); silken: simple (l. 364); on: o'er (l. 596). That these are aural and not visual errors is clear from the second and third pairs: *silken* has no descenders, and *o'er* is double the length of *on.* The first two errors do not destroy the sense, but they do weaken it.

These particular errors are easily discovered by the fact that more correct manuscripts of the same poem exist. Ideally, we should have the corrected manuscripts of any author to print from, but even in such a case, we may be momentarily misled, as when Wordsworth, following his broad, north-country pronunciation, spells *note, nought.*[1] That this is not a single accident is shown by the rime *remote-thought* in the *Death of a Starling.*

A suspicious nature is an asset to the textual critic. Often he will be led to examine a passage because the meaning is not quite clear, and he will not be dazzled by the authority of the edition in hand. Thus, in a recent textbook, he will find this line in Browning's *In a Gondola:*

Past every church that saints and saves.

Surely that makes only a sort of sense. Browning could scarcely be talking of canonization, and it is unusual

[1] *Early Letters,* ed. E. de Selincourt, p. 77. See also *Poetical Works,* ed. de Selincourt, I, 367.

for him to use a word so loosely. Back to the first edition, and we read:

> Past every church that sains and saves,

that is, purifies or cleanses, which is excellent. (It might be interpolated at this point that many of the nineteenth-century poets are much more in need of careful textual editing than they are of extensive explanatory annotation.)

The textual critic will not allow the accepted clichés of criticism to relieve him of firsthand examination of the work concerned. When Shelley's *Laon and Cythna,* already printed, was felt to be too objectionable for publication without extensive changes, cancels were introduced and changes made. Shelley explained these in a letter to Moore as follows: "The present edition of 'Laon and Cythna' is to be suppressed, and it will be republished in about a fortnight under the title of 'The Revolt of Islam,' with some alterations which consist in little else than the substitution of the words *friend* or *lover* for that of *brother* and *sister.*" Even the latest and best biographer, Professor White, does little but paraphrase this: "The bulk of the revisions had to do with changing the relationship of Laon and Cythna from brother and sister to cousins." Examination of the changes shows both statements to be totally misleading. Actually, Shelley made alterations in forty-three passages, a total of sixty-two lines. Of these, only eight changes, of eleven lines, concern the incestuous relationship. But thirty-three changes of forty-nine lines soften the sharp atheistical tone of the early version. Two other changes are stylistic. In other words, the changes as to religion are four times as numerous and four times as extensive as the others. I might add that seven of the first eight changes do concern incest. Can it be that the biographers looked no further?

Sometimes a careful comparative study of early texts has a consequence beyond the immediate meaning of a passage. Coleridge repeatedly insisted that *Kubla Khan* was written down just as it came to him in his dream, and immediately upon awakening. His usually careful editor, J. Dykes Campbell, contradicted this story by printing some lines by Mrs. "Perdita" Robinson, written in 1800, sixteen years before the poem was published, in a complimentary poem to Coleridge, published in 1801. These purported to contain three quotations from the poem, as follows:

> I'll mark thy "sunny dome," and view
> Thy "caves of ice," thy "fields of dew."

The first two appear in the published poem; the "fields of dew" do not.

Campbell inferred from this couplet that Mrs. Robinson had seen an earlier manuscript, and hence that the poem as printed is not the poem as originally written down, and, given his evidence, such an inference is inevitable. He was followed by E. H. Coleridge, also an able editor. But Lowes was not satisfied, and looked up the volume from which Campbell quoted, where he found the couplet printed without quotation marks around "fields of dew." [2] Mrs. Robin-

[2] *The Road to Xanadu*, p. 354.

son probably introduced the phrase because of exigencies of rime. The couplet contains no variants, and hence the hypothesis of an earlier manuscript falls to the ground. It is clear then that Coleridge did tell the truth—at least no evidence exists to the contrary—and the poem as it stands is a dream poem, and not a work of art in the ordinary sense.

Three variants do exist in the present text, but they are of no importance, each involving a single letter only: the first may perhaps be due to degeneration of the text from printers' errors: *here* for *there*. Since the word occurs in the middle of the line, the initial *t* may have dropped out without being noticed. Either word makes good sense, but I feel that Coleridge wrote *there*. It is possible that after the appearance of the third edition he changed the word to enforce a parallelism with *here* two lines below. The passage reads:

And *there* were gardens bright in sinuous rills,
　Where blossomed many an incense-bearing tree;
And *here* were forests ancient as the hills
　Enfolding sunny spots of greenery.[3]

Enfolding is the second variant, originally *And folding*, which is nonsense, apparently a misreading from dictation. (Capital *A* and *E* can scarcely be mistaken in reading, and *d* is too distinctive a letter to be omitted.) The third may well be due to Coleridge: the grammar is corrected by changing *drank* to *drunk* in the last line of the poem; but there is no reason to think Coleridge

[3] Italics supplied. See also *T.L.S.*, 1934, p. 541.

did not first write *drank*. *Drunk* looks like a correction of sobriety.

Another type of textual problem arises from a printer's misreading of an author's manuscript. This is rather uncommon; printers show an amazing ability to read difficult handwriting. In Dr. Johnson's *London* the first five editions read:

> Fair Justice then, without constraint ador'd
>   Sustain'd the Ballance, but resign'd the Sword.

When the poem was reprinted in Dodsley's *Collection*, the second line was changed to read:

> Held high the steady scale, but deep'd the sword.

Johnson evidently felt that his intention was not accurately rendered by having Justice *resign* the sword, but what does the new reading mean? As far as is known, this was Johnson's last revision of the poem; and inasmuch as it was printed in an anthology, he is not likely to have seen proofs. No use of *deep* as a verb is recorded in Johnson's *Dictionary*, nor is any meaning assignable to the word here. I believe that the printer misread *drop'd*, which, with both *r* and *o* open in Dr. Johnson's most perplexing hand, is easily converted into *deep'd*, especially since he uses two types of *e* indiscriminately. *Drop'd* makes good sense here. It is the technical language of fencing, to drop the point, which was common in the eighteenth century, and is still. The general meaning of the passage, then, is that in the Golden Age, Justice, while still maintaining her scales, will not require the sword to enforce her edicts: but she merely relaxes the maintenance of force by dropping the point of the sword, not giving up the possible recourse to force.[4]

At this point I ought to say that the conscientious textual critic, while anxious to come as close to the author's text as may be, will never help the author to write it. He will not make changes just to improve grammar, as has been frequently done in Shelley's poems by W. M. Rossetti and occasionally even by Professor Woodberry, who in one instance gives this curious explanation of an emendation:

Conducts, Rossetti thus corrects the original reading, *conduct,* which is, however, retained by all other editors. Shelley doubtless wrote *conduct,* the verb being attracted into the plural by the number of details mentioned in connection with *vault;* other explanations, on the ground of *does* understood, in one or another way, are only ingenious excuses; the structure of the group of questions is so continuous that it seems best to make the change.[5]

Nor will a strict editor try to give a tight and logical structure to a passage which is loose and rambling but makes generally good sense. For example, half a dozen emendations have been proposed, by Rossetti, Swinburne, Forman, and others, for the following lines from *Alastor:*

On every side now rose
Rocks, which, in unimaginable forms,
Lifted their black and barren pinnacles

[4] Hawkins in 1787 gives a new reading:

        Held high the steady scale, but sheath'd the sword.

This cuts the Gordian knot. I suspect that it is an alternative reading rejected by Johnson during the revision of the poem. It is worse than the other two.

[5] Cambridge ed., p. 615.

In the light of evening, and its precipice
Obscuring the ravine, disclosed above,
'Mid toppling stones, black gulfs and yawning caves . . .

[ll. 543–8]

The only genuine difficulty is that Shelley first takes *rocks* plurally and then collectively, with a consequent *its*. No emendation is required or justified.

A word may be said concerning correction of punctuation. During most of English literary history, I believe punctuation has been largely determined by printing-house practice. Sometimes a meticulous author has been able to force his eccentricities upon the printer, but that is unusual. Nevertheless, I believe that the textual critic should show great caution in emending punctuation, where no manuscript exists. Even if the author did not himself do the pointing, he was satisfied that it did no violence to his meaning, or he would have changed it. An extreme example of this is Byron, who left such matters to Gifford, Murray's advisor. Unless the editor can show that the pointing is obviously wrong, he ought to let it alone. If he thinks it confusing, he can indicate an improvement in the notes.

Occasionally the alert textual critic will become aware of a textual flaw because of faulty rhythm. In the best modern text of Browning, the following lines occur in the *Soliloquy of the Spanish Cloister:*

If I trip him just a-dying,
    Sure of heaven as sure as can be,
Spin him round, and send him flying
    Off to hell, a Manichee?

There is no serious fault of sense, though the second line appears both loose and ugly, particularly in rhythm. Reference to early editions of Browning shows that he wrote the line without the second *as:*

> Sure of heaven as sure can be.

On the other hand, a scrupulous editor will not casually correct the rhythm of a passage he believes faulty. Paul Elmer More decided that a line in Byron's *Don Juan* (V, st. 55) was imperfect. It reads:

> As wondering what the devil noise that is.

Mr. More inserted an *a* before *noise,* with this comment: "The scansion shows that the common text has some such omission." [6] My scansion shows nothing of the sort, and if it did, I should be inclined to comment that it is Byron's poem.

The textual critic will use all the aids of bibliography. If he is to print from a first edition, he will have to know what issue it is. Otherwise, he may find, in printing from the first issue of *Lyrical Ballads,* 1800, instead of the second, that he has omitted fifteen lines of *Michael,* and committed other blunders perhaps less important, but more difficult to detect. He will be wary of forgeries, and watch watermarks, because the forgery is a step away from the original, and the watermarks may show up tell-tale cancels or made-up copies.

From the examples I have cited, I should now like to proceed to some general principles. It may be taken as axiomatic, I think, that textual degeneration is an

6 Cambridge ed., pp. 838, 1036.

almost inevitable process, if reference is not constantly
made to the first editions and manuscripts. Printers'
and editors' errors creep in, generation after generation. Efforts to solve textual cruces without reference
to prime sources usually add to the degeneration, and
at best are merely lucky guesses. The textual critic
must make his tools of learning as various as possible.
As my examples indicate, he should be familiar with
the handwriting of the author whom he is studying.
He should also try to understand dialectal peculiarities
of his author's speech, which may be shown in the
author's spelling, or reflected in the words taken down
in dictation. He should, in case of a manuscript, determine whether it contains evidence of dictation. He
must, in addition to these things, familiarize himself
with all pertinent biographical data. For example, did
the author read his own proofs? (Wordsworth did not,
for the 1800 *Lyrical Ballads.*) Who read them for him?
What latitude was granted in proof revision? Can any
readings be ascribed to an editor? In posthumously
published work, what editorial supervision was exer-
cised? (See Mr. de Selincourt on the publication of
Wordsworth's *Prelude.*) In case of two extant versions
of the same work, which is the later? Which was the
author's preference? Not necessarily the later. If the
earlier is the better, as with Keats's *Hyperion,* the
editor should publish both, and often it is instructive
to do so in any case.

Ideally, the textual scholar should be omniscient,
and endowed, in addition, with endless energy and

general skepticism. If he lacks some or all of these qualities, at least in the highest degree, perhaps he will console himself with Chaucer's wise observation:

The lyf so short, the craft so long to lerne.

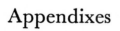

Appendixes

Supervising Committee, 1946

Evening Lectures

The English Institute

II. THE CRITICAL SIGNIFICANCE OF BIO-
GRAPHICAL EVIDENCE
SEPTEMBER 10–13, at 10:45 A.M.
Directed by GERALD E. BENTLEY, *Princeton University*

1. John Milton
   DOUGLAS BUSH, *Harvard University*

2. Jonathan Swift
   LOUIS A. LANDA, *Princeton University*

3. Percy Bysshe Shelley
   CARLOS H. BAKER, *Princeton University*

4. William Butler Yeats
   MARION WITT, *Hunter College*

III. FACSIMILES, FORGERIES, AND REPRINTS
SEPTEMBER 10–13, at 1:30 P.M.
Directed by ALLEN T. HAZEN, *University of Chicago*

1. Procedures in Verifying Questioned Documents
   ALBERT D. OSBORN, *Examiner of Questioned Documents, New York*

2. Early Forgeries in Manuscripts and Printed
   Books
   CURT F. BÜHLER, *Morgan Library*

3. Type-Facsimiles
   ALLEN T. HAZEN, *University of Chicago*

4. Modern Forgeries of Shelley's Checks
   ROBERT M. SMITH, *Lehigh University*

IV. THE METHODS OF LITERARY STUDIES
SEPTEMBER 10–13, at 3:00 P.M.
Directed by ARTHUR MIZENER, *Carleton College*

1. Textual Scholarship
   EDWARD L. MCADAM, JR., *New York University*

2. Acting and Stage History
   ALAN S. DOWNER, *Princeton University*

3. Literary History
   RENÉ WELLEK, *Yale University*

4. Literary Criticism
   CLEANTH BROOKS, *Louisiana State University*

Registrants

GELLERT S. ALLEMAN
Lehigh University

RICHARD D. ALTICK
Ohio State University

DOROTHY C. ALYEA
*Adult Education School
Montclair, New Jersey*

MARCIA LEE ANDERSON
Hollins College

MARJORIE ANDERSON
Hunter College

GEORGE W. ARMS
University of New Mexico

CARLOS H. BAKER
Princeton University

ALBERT C. BAUGH
University of Pennsylvania

ROLAND BAUGHMAN
Columbia University

REV. PAUL E. BEICHNER,
C.S.C.
University of Notre Dame

JOSEPHINE WATERS BEN-
NETT
Hunter College

ALICE R. BENSEN
Valparaiso University

GERALD E. BENTLEY
Princeton University

DOROTHY BETHURUM
Connecticut College

WERNER W. BEYER
Rutgers University

FREDERIKA BLANKNER
Adelphi College

LOUISE SCHUTZ BOAS
Wheaton College

MURIEL BOWDEN
405 Park Avenue, New York City

ALICE S. BRANDENBURG
Wilson College

MARY CAMPBELL BRILL
*102 East 31st Street, New York
City*

CLEANTH BROOKS
Louisiana State University

MARGARET M. BRYANT
Brooklyn College

CURT F. BÜHLER
Pierpont Morgan Library

KATHERINE BURTON
Wheaton College

DOUGLAS BUSH
Harvard University

FRANK M. CALDIERO
Cooper Union

ALBERT HOWARD CARTER
Folger Shakespeare Library

CATHERINE CATER
Olivet College

DONALD L. CLARK
Columbia University

JAMES L. CLIFFORD
Columbia University

GEORGE R. COFFMAN
University of North Carolina

RALPH L. COLLINS
Indiana University

MARJORIE D. COOGAN
Barnard College

THOMAS W. COPELAND
Yale University

V. MIGNON COUSER
Foxcroft

REV. JOHN V. CURRY, S.J.
Fordham University

CARL E. W. L. DAHLSTRÖM
University of Michigan

ELLEN DAVIDSON
University of Chicago

LLOYD J. DAVIDSON
University of Chicago

GILES E. DAWSON
Folger Shakespeare Library

SARA DE FORD
Goucher College

CHARLOTTE D'EVELYN
Mount Holyoke College

ALAN S. DOWNER
Princeton University

JEREMIAH K. DURICK
St. Michael's College

IRVIN EHRENPREIS
Indiana University

GEORGE J. ENGELHARDT
University of Connecticut

WILLA McC. EVANS
Hunter College

CHARLES K. EVES
City College of New York

LAVINIA B. EVES
Hunter College

OLOF VON FEILITZEN
Royal Library, Stockholm

JOHN H. FISHER
New York University

EDWARD G. FLETCHER
University of Texas

FRANK CUDWORTH FLINT
Dartmouth College

STEPHEN F. FOGLE
University of Florida

FRANCES A. FOSTER
Vassar College

J. MILTON FRENCH
Rutgers University

HORST FRENZ
Indiana University

ALBERT FRIEND
City College of New York

KATHERINE HAYNES GATCH
Hunter College

MARY E. GIFFIN
Vassar College

ROBERTA M. GRAHAME
Wellesley College

RICHARD L. GREENE
Wells College

H. PEARSON GUNDY
Mount Allison University

GORDON S. HAIGHT
Yale University

EVELYN A. HANLEY
Adelphi College

JULIA HAMLET HARRIS
Meredith College

RUTH MACK HAVENS
New Paltz State Teachers College

ALLEN T. HAZEN
University of Chicago

ATCHESON L. HENCH
University of Virginia

CHARLTON HINMAN
Johns Hopkins University

HELEN HOTCHKISS
Hunter College

CECILIA A. HOTCHNER
Hunter College

GEORGE W. HOWGATE
Marshall College

MURIEL J. HUGHES
University of Vermont

ELEANOR HYDE
Barnard College

GENE IRVINE
Columbia University

WILLIAM ROBERT IRWIN
Cornell University

A. R. JEWITT
University of Western Ontario

LISLE C. JOHN
Hunter College

CHARLES W. JONES
Cornell University

JOYCE L. KELLOGG
Western Reserve University

LUCILE W. KENNEDY
Columbia University

MARJORIE M. KIMMERLE
University of Colorado

JOHN P. KIRBY
Mary Washington College

RUDOLF KIRK
Rutgers University

MARY E. KNAPP
Albertus Magnus College

DOROTHY ALDEN KOCH
Bryn Mawr College

KATHRINE KOLLER
University of Rochester

JAMES CRAIG LA DRIÈRE
Catholic University

LOUIS A. LANDA
Princeton University

STEPHEN A. LARRABEE
Waterville, Maine

BABETTE MAY LEVY
Hunter College

JEAN S. LINDSAY
Hunter College

JULIAN I. LINDSAY
University of Vermont

FRANCIS E. LITZ
Catholic University

LOUIS G. LOCKE
Southwestern University

HELEN H. LOVE
Hunter College

CAROLINE S. LUTZ
Westhampton College

THOMAS O. MABBOTT
Hunter College

EDWARD L. MCADAM, JR.
New York University

INA BETH MCGAVOCK
Trinity University

WILLIAM MCGAVOCK
San Antonio, Texas

CLAIRE MCGLINCHEE
Hunter College

ALAN D. MCKILLOP
Rice Institute

ALICE K. MCLARNEY
Hunter College

HELEN NEILL MCMASTER
Sarah Lawrence College

ELIZABETH W. MANWARING
Wellesley College

MARY HATCH MARSHALL
Colby College

THOMAS F. MARSHALL, III
Western Maryland College

VALENTINE MERIVALE
*244 East 55th Street, New York
City*

LAURENCE A. MICHEL, JR.
Yale University

FRANCIS E. MINEKA
Cornell University

LOUIE M. MINER
Brooklyn College

CHARLES C. MISH
University of Pennsylvania

RUTH MOHL
Brooklyn College

SAMUEL H. MONK
Box 25, Princeton, New Jersey

CHARLOTTE E. MORGAN
Brooklyn College

ELIZABETH NITCHIE
Goucher College

MILDRED NOBLE
Mount Holyoke College

LUELLA F. NORWOOD
Colby College

ALBERT D. OSBORN
233 Broadway, New York City

NORMAN HOLMES PEARSON
Yale University

KATHRYN KING PEASE
Chapin School

HARRY WILLIAM PEDICORD
University of Pennsylvania

KATHERINE H. PORTER
Western Reserve University

ABBIE FINDLAY POTTS
Rockford College

ESTHER M. POWER
Arlington, Virginia

HEREWARD T. PRICE
University of Michigan

MAURICE J. QUINLAN
Lehigh University

REV. CHARLES J. QUIRK, S.J.
Loyola University of the South

ISABEL E. RATHBORNE
Hunter College

ALLEN WALKER READ
Columbia University

GERTRUDE B. RIVERS
Howard University

DAVID ALLAN ROBERTSON, JR.
Barnard College

HELEN E. SANDISON
Vassar College

ROSEMARIE SCHAWLOW
University of Toronto

HELENE B. M. SCHNABEL
390 Wadsworth Avenue, New York City

RAYMOND W. SHORT
Hofstra College

SISTER MARY AQUINAS DEVLIN
Rosary College

SISTER TERESA MARIE FARRELL
St. Joseph's College for Women

SAMUEL A. SMALL
West Virginia Wesleyan College

REV. PAUL F. SMITH, S.J.
Creighton University

ROBERT M. SMITH
Lehigh University

H. M. SMYSER
Connecticut College

NATHAN C. STARR
Rollins College

TRUMAN G. STEFFAN
University of Texas

RANDALL STEWART
Brown University

ELEANOR W. THOMAS
Western Reserve University

WILLARD THORP
Princeton University

JAMES E. THORPE, JR.
Princeton University

ADELINE R. TINTNER
140 East 46th Street, New York City

JAMES E. TOBIN
Tuckahoe, New York

ANNA M. TRINSEY
Hunter College

ROSEMOND TUVE
Connecticut College

EMMA V. UNGER
Carl H. Pforzheimer Library

JEANNETTE VAN ARENDONK
New Paltz State Teachers College

CONSTANCE SOUTHARD VEY-SEY
Hunter College

HOWARD P. VINCENT
Illinois Institute of Technology

EUGENE M. WAITH
Yale University

RENÉ WELLEK
Yale University

HAROLD WENTWORTH
Temple University

PHILIP WHEELWRIGHT
Dartmouth College

EDNA R. WILLIAMS
Smith College

EDWIN E. WILLOUGHBY
Folger Shakespeare Library

MILDRED WILSEY
Wilson College

MARION WITT
Hunter College

ERNEST HUNTER WRIGHT
Columbia University

MARY A. WYMAN
Hunter College

Index

Index

Index

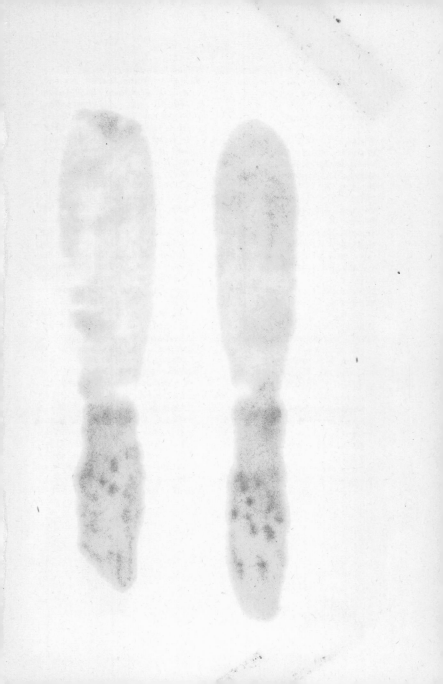